RELIGION AND CONTEMPORARY ART ESSAYS (2001-2005)

By Anthony Padgett

Published by
The Auditors of God

First Published 2010
Copyright Anthony Padgett 2010

ISBN 978-0-9561587-3-4

TABLE OF CONTENTS

Dedicated to
Stephanie Sturges

Cover Picture: "The Eve II Revelation" 2003,
acrylic on canvas, 120cm x 80cm, Anthony Padgett.

PREFACE

Anthony Padgett has a BA in Philosophy, a PGCE in Teaching Religious Education, a PG Diploma in Conservation of Architectural Stone and an MA in Theory of Contemporary Art & Performance.

From 1995 -1999 he worked with the British School of Archaeology in Jerusalem, the Israeli Antiquities Authority, the Palestinian Department of Antiquities, Lancaster University Archaeological Unit and the Historic American Buildings Survey, Washington D.C.

From 1999-2005 his art was in numerous group and solo exhibitions, and he was an Artist-in-Residence at Loughborough University, the winner of the About Vision Art & Technology Award (London), a finalist in the International Jewish Artist of the Year Award 2004, an A-foundation commissioned artist for Liverpool Biennial 2004 and a performer at Edinburgh Fringe 2005.

His work has been featured in the Guardian, the Mail on Sunday, Times Online, Times Educational Supplement and BBC Radio 4. He has given talks about contemporary religious art at various venues, including the New York Studio School of Art, the Institute of Contemporary Art and Tate Modern.

This book is a collection of the essays of Padgett, written following the art projects that he created from 1994 and the exhibitions that he had held from 1999. This was part of an exploration, a journey, a quest to find the relationship between art and religion, which he began as a youth in 1985 and which he completed in his most recent work, his novel "The Rainbow Swastika Conspiracy", 2006-9

The first part of this collection of essays is from 2001-2002. It consists of essays about "The Ism", his art practice from 1994-2001. These ideas were crystallised around 1999-2000. Here Padgett seeks to unite different religious and spiritual perspectives by finding the artforms most appropriate to them (with sculpture relating to Western religions and installations and performance relating to Eastern spirituality) and then uniting the artforms. Within this unity he seeks to place immanent duality above universal non-duality.

The second part of this collection consists of essays from 2002-2005 in a period when Padgett studied at Wimbledon School of Art, London, for an MA in Theory of Contemporary Art and Performance. They contain writings about other contemporary artists and here Padgett develops the notion of "Postmodern Religious Art". Here his program of uniting the artforms is progressed by his attempts to unite the specifics of religions with the general spiritual universals principles that pervade contemporary art. He also seeks to unite the sacred and the profane – but always placing religion and the specific as of greater importance. Thus finding a solution to his need to place immanent duality above universal non-duality.

The final part of this collection consists of the questionnaire that Padgett submitted to the Employment Tribunals, concerning his belief that the Tate Galleries were exercising religious discrimination in the way that they selected artworks. This questionnaire gives the main arguments behind this claim.

After 2 years this case was rejected on a technicality so Padgett rejected the artworld as being corrupt and his project of Postmodern Religious Art as having failed. So he put his final writings into a novel form, believing that this best captured the essence of true religious art. In the novel he argues that the book is the highest expression of religion, for example the Bible, the Koran, the Bhagavad Gita, the Guru Granth Sahib. He has also published images of his art and performance in a number of books.

In Essay 1 **"Reconciling Binary Oppositions"** Padgett argues that opposing artistic expressions directly show a conflict between Moral and Mystical Consciousness. He describes his computer based artwork and his deliberate contrast between figurative sculpture and abstract installations as an instance of this. He then describes how he plans to make a synthesis of these in artistic rituals. Padgett then describes his philosophical ideas on the nature of creativity. He describes the shaping of abstract energy into figurative form. In the final part of this essay he describes how this relationship between the two consciousnesses has manifest itself in cultural history. Finally he gives a list of opposites that he proposes to link in his art movement named The-Ism.

In Essay 2 **"East Meets West Philosophically Through Art & Performance"** Padgett attempts to move away from postmodern relativism by making a map of world religions and their art forms. He intends that this map would enable an analysis of underlying trends and how contradictions can be united into a dynamic relativism between two perspectives. The visual art section is illustrated with his Game of World Religious Art and the performing art section with his Disco Art Religion rituals and parties.

In Essay 3 **"The Postmodern Art Work Of Jake And Dinos Chapman - Situated With Reference To Young British Art (YBA)"** Padgett argues that Fascist art was concerned with classical form and avant-garde communist art was more concerned with formlessness and breaking down structure. He argues that the work of the YBAs links to the Nazis in their glorification of the local and the national but also links to Bakhtin's Carnival and a Universal Formless. Padgett contends that the Chapmans aim to completely break down moral and intellectual structures in order to achieve a different perspective. However the majority of people will always view the work from a moral perspective and miss this breaking down and as such the Chapman's work is elitist. The Chapmans laughingly play into attention seeking but also have a serious point.

In Essay 4 **"Is Artaud's Inclusive Theatre Really Exclusive?"** Padgett relates Anton Artaud's "Theatre of Cruelty", that encompasses the audience within the performance, to a Gnostic conception of the universe where Artaud is fighting against the notion of a creator God/demi-urge. Padgett constrasts Nietzsche's and Artuad's views of God to show how the Gnostic viewpoint differs from a traditional Western perspective. Derrida's *notion of* Artaud's art being without works is discussed in relation to this. Sontag criticises Artuad's work as being personal and non-political but Baker-White argues for the communal nature of Artaud's theatre. The contradictory notions of community and individuality in Artaud's work are viewed as creating a paradox of rationality. Padgett proposes that Artuad sought to transcend this paradox in a Gnostic non-dualism that goes beyond classifications such as inclusive and exclusive. "The Singularity", a performance by Foolishpeople, is discussed in relation to its success in transforming the audience through Artaudian "Theatre of Cruelty" and Gnosticism.

In Essay 5 **"The Art And Performance Of Anthony Padgett"** Padgett describe the objectives and methodologies of his own practice and then situates this with reference to broader religious, social, historical, curatorial and political questions. He looks at how the work corresponds with other artists' work and what function it has in society. Due to the breadth of his practice he restricts this comparison to the work of three practitioners. The sculpture of Jake & Dinos Chapman, the performance of the Blue Man Group and, for a combination of the two, the work of Revd Ethan Acres. To conclude he offers some artistic and political criticisms of these works.

In Essay 6 **"The Relation Between Theory And Practice Of The Work Of Thomas Hirschhorn With Specific Reference To Art And Popular Culture"** Padgett focuses on Thomas Hirschhorn, who investigates the end of utopian thinking but celebrates the energy of utopian thinkers. His installations use a chaos of everyday materials and rubbish in order to emphasise process, to reject ideological closure and to link to the in*forme* and rejects consumerism. Stallabras criticises artworks like these for not being critical but Roberts sees them as a critique of ineffective critical thinking. Beech and Roberts suggest that the notion of the Philistine allows culture to shift but Stallabras thinks it gives licence to be uncritical. Quinn suggests that notion of the Philistine reintroduces critical thought. Whilst Krishnan and Harvey propose a critical and regulatory base can arise for culture the work of Hirschhorn does not envisage this. Padgett proposes that the origin of the term Philistine is Palestine and that Islam is seen as a modern philistinism that addresses critical thinking and provides a way out of the lack of critical direction.

In Essay 7 **"What Are The Possibilities For Postmodern Religious Art?"** Padgett looks at trends in contemporary religious art focussing on the work of Damien Hirst, Gomez Pena, Lionello Borean and Shilpa Gupta. He then fits these within modernist and postmodern perspectives. He differentiates between modernist certainty of progress towards Utopian aspirations and a postmodern uncertainty. He posits that Postmodern Religious Art is not deconstructive or nihilistic but is constructive and involves rituals and artworks that express a semi-ironic faith in "Divine Intervention". Such an approach focuses on the gods and institutional, outer forms of religion whereas, he argues, art theorists have preferred spiritual, aesthetic expressions.

In Essay **8 "Postmodern Religious Art – From Liminality To Messianicity"** Padgett seeks to give a structure for understanding and situating the use of religious imagery in contemporary art. He looks at how modernists rejected traditional religion in favour our atheism or spirituality. He then sees how postmodernists reinstate religious concerns, but in a commodified, superficial and pluralistic way. He argues that despite this apparent secularisation genuine religious sentiments can still be produced by such work. Finally he examines examples of postmodern religious art to explain the proposed definition.

Essay **9 "A Definition Of Postmodern Religious Art"** is a definition that Padgett posted onto Wikipedia. It situates the movement in relation to pre-modernism, modernism, Late-Capitalism and the avant-garde.

The final essay 10 is the **Questionnaire** that Padgett sent to the Employment Tribunal Sir Nicholas Serota and Tate Galleries over Religious Discrimination under The Employment Equality (Religion or Belief) Regulations 2003. The Tribunal case was a piece of art and an attempt to take control of state funded art away from corporate collectors and commercial galleries by protecting artists/performers rights (disability, race, sex, sexual orientation, age and religion). He sought to resist the culture of multinational collectors and their spreading globalisation. The case had implications for the UK and also for Europe as the EE Regulations 2003 are formulated out of the EU Employment Framework Directive (Directive 2000/78).

02 February 2010

10

Early Essays (2001-2002)
"The Ism" / "Theism"

Essay 1.

RECONCILING BINARY OPPOSITIONS

1. ART DIRECTLY EXPRESSING A CONFLICT BETWEEN TWO CONSCIOUSNESSES

Moral and Mystical Consciousness

Immanuel Kant gave antinomies relating to space and time in the Critique of Pure Reason. These antinomies are mutually contradictory propositions each of which can apparently be proved, a thesis and an antithesis, eg whether we should think that matter is made of indivisible atoms or as infinitely divisible. My work resembles this mapping of opposites but my binary oppositions are in terms of art forms and ways of perception. The conclusion of my work tries to synthesise these opposites. The work is a conceptual art project, called The Ism (www.theism.co.uk), that I exhibited at 4 solo shows in London, 2000-2001. The oppositions are characterised as being black and white for purposes of argument and are not meant as an absolute statement.

The split between the two ways of perceiving is between mystical non-dualism and moral dualism. The mystical links to a primal, eternal, experiential Energy. The moral links to the conceptual structure that gives Form to the Energy, via creativity. The split is also between Jungian Transcendence (going beyond dual conception to non-dual experience) and Freudian Sublimation (moving from one duality to a higher duality, eg. from the sexual to the spiritual).

Primal Energy relates to nature and the form that shapes this energy relates to technology. Nature is often figuratively represented in art however the underlying principle of nature is as an abstract mystical, process that follows rational laws. Technology may seem very abstract, however the underlying principle is figurative as it concerns the human will and faith in the mastery of nature through technological means.

This split between Nature and Technology is also the split between the Dionysian and the Apollonian. Nature is Dionysian and is a timeless and cyclical, process. In this perspective human beings are intimately connected with nature as there is no subject or object distinction. Technology is Apollonian, progressive and orientated toward an end product or goal. In this perspective computers have been used to industrially manufacture objects external to the subject.

Both of these perspectives also incorporate their opposite. An Apollonian view of nature is figurative and nature is represented as an external product with mind and matter seen as separate. A Dionysian use of technology and computers is in socially interactive art installations and world-wide communications. This use breaks down the subject-object distinction in a pantheistic way.

Abstract nature is closer to mystical non-dualism and abstract interactive art links to this. Figurative technology is built out of the abstract elements and is closer to the dualism of human, moral will and figurative art links to this.

These 2 perspectives cannot be reconciled so the human mind often accepts one of these opposites and rejects the other. Part of my art work is to contrast the use of computers in interactive abstract installations and their use in exclusive figurative computer manufactured sculpture. This is so that I can then link the two together as a way to link the mystical and moral consciousnesses.

Opposing Artistic Expressions

Through 1990 – 1994 I had been keeping a sculpture diary of my journey to find spiritual meaning when I had a mystical experience. After meditating I entered a mystical, non-dual state of consciousness that is experiential, prior to concepts and is beyond meaning and meaninglessness. In contrast, moral spirituality is conceptual and dualistic (ie there is a focus on opposites like good and evil, subject and object).

Prior to the mind's application of dualistic concepts things are experienced as immediate and without any greater significance. Because there is no self conscious differentiation everything is seen as being of the same basic, ordinary, nature and consciousness is universally and timelessly the same as everything. As soon as I became self conscious (subject-object) in this state the experience dissolved away.

I became aware that mystical consciousness could not solve my moral problems, just dissolves the duality that is the basis of the problems. The two consciousnesses are distinct and irreconcilable philosophically but I felt that there had to be some common ground between them as I had experienced some continuity of identity and memory between the mind states.

Advanced mystics synthesise these opposites by experiencing duality whilst in a non-dualistic consciousness but this duality is never directly experienced. It is always seen as secondary, illusory and unreal. Mystics claim to have a link but they ignore how the mystical consciousness remains in a binary opposition to normal consciousness. The dualist can try to incorporate the mystical into their life by seeing it as a separate consciousness. This maintains the two experiences as separate and avoids the dual being subsumed under the non-dual as an illusion, however the two are never directly linked.

This question of whether illusion (duality) is included in enlightenment or whether it is separated has been a conundrum for Hindu and Buddhist scholars with different schools emphasising different conclusions. Of the question the Buddha said that it is one of a number of dualistic questions not worth asking as they are not conducive to the very practical issue of reaching a non-dualistic enlightenment experience.

Whilst I was consciously struggling with these philosophical issues I began to unconsciously reconcile the two perspectives in art. Later I saw a pattern emerging and began to consciously develop this reconciliation. By joining the art forms to their appropriate perspective and then linking the art forms together a link was made between the two perspectives (in a single piece of art) that could not be made philosophically. I tried to accept both the opposites and live with the division with the art form as a way of reconciliation that was both experientially and conceptually apprehended.

Computer Expressionism

After my mystical experience I found that I began to have another, non-sculptural, form of artistic expression relating to art therapy and abstract expressionism. This form of expression embodied primal energy and non-dual experience. The work involved the energy of the participants without their consciously imposing form on the work. I conducted an abstract expressionist experiment that involved wilfully drawing, but without imposing any ideas of style, form or composition on the creative process. The hope was that eventually universal forms of design would arise naturally out of this chaotic energy and that these designs would be therapeutic.

4 artists made 10 drawings each on a computer drawing board. The drawing area was 130cm wide by 100cm high and was 100cm above the ground. Sensors on red, green and blue pens allowed for the plotting of the pens' movements and the recording of the drawing. Drawings were recorded in real time and were played back at different speeds and digitally separated into their 3 colours. Each drawing was made after a period of meditation and was only viewed at the end of the experiment. Personality tests (Eysenck) were used to see how psychology type related to the drawing styles.

A common pattern emerged. All the initial drawings had conflicting elements (eg arcs and scribbles) that began to be unconsciously synthesised as the experiment progressed. The 2 males filled the drawing area and the 2 females worked within constructed boundaries. All participants had similar psychological scores but the participant that had been self-conscious (and not immediate) when producing the work scored high on the check to see if questions were being answered self-consciously. No firm conclusions can be drawn from the experiment and it is just a prototype for a larger experiment. Possible implications, however, are that the mind looks for unity and order and that males are more exploratory and outgoing than females who are more protective.

The "White"board was used as part of my artist-in-residency at Loughborough University with the C&CRS for COSTART, partly funded by the EPSRC Grant GR/M14517 Studies of Computer

Support for Creative Work, Artists and Technologists in Collaboration. Work with the 3 other artists was AA2A supported by Arts Council Lottery funding.

Outside of this experiment my own expressionistic work eventually evolved through circular expressive scribbles into the ancient mystical symbols of the swastika and the rainbow. This symbol also unconsciously arose in my computer installation (see later). The swastika relates to the mystical theosophical movement that Jung and the Modern artists Mondrian and Kandinsky were involved in. I am Jewish and am aware of its Nazi connotations but the symbol is also a cross-cultural spiritual symbol.

Computer Sculpture

Meanwhile in my sculpture diary I was unconsciously finding some resolution for the split in my consciousness by symbolically re-creating the conflict in sculptures (abstract, mystical metal and figurative, moral wood) and then bringing these opposing sculptural elements together.

The sculptures that I will focus on here are those manufactured by computers. These are from the technological and figurative part of my sculptural work.

These sculptural works stand separate from nature. They relate to humanity, to Form imposed upon matter, and to moral, dual, meaningful, conceptual structures.

These sculptures are about a historical progress to reach an end goal and a static product. They move from Greek and Zoroastrian imagery to images of Islam and to a Millennium art event at the Golden Gate in Jerusalem.

The 2D work Apollo vs Dionysus shows an abstract design in contrast with a 3D laser scan of a sculpture of the head of Apollo that I carved in stone. The work shows the figurative art arising from the abstract design. The selfish, individualistic ego (head of Apollo) separates from the infinite mystical background through self-consciousness. Apollo also represents Greek philosophy and conceptual dualism.

The Zoroastrian Icarus was made as £150,000 sponsorship from 15 UK companies. A 30 centimeter original stone sculpture (that I had hand carved in stone) was laser & probe scanned then manufactured at 2 metres high by Stereolithography (SLA), Layer Object Manufacture (LOM) and Computer Numerate Controlled (CNC) machining. It is currently being bronze cast and has been displayed at numerous international computer manufacturing shows - see www.millennium-angel.co.uk

The ancient and the futuristic are linked in this symbol of an individual's trying to reach beyond himself to master nature by technology. References are made to the historical tradition of Monotheism and its influence from the hierarchical dualism of Zoroastrianism and also to the free thought of Greek philosophy. The assumptions that the nature of technology is as an abstract process was also questioned in the work as laser scanning had increased the ease of manufacturing figurative products.

This individual attempt at mastery over nature was sublimated into a communal co-operation in the circle of 7 figures called Islam. This was made from one computer file (AutoCAD drawing) that was then machined by LOM. Each figure was then cast in resin as a colour of the rainbow. The dominant individual had become communally symbolised as a repeat copy from an immaterial Platonic Form. The spiritual meaning was now found in community and love, and not in the individual.

This sublimation to higher figurative expression was taken to its conclusion in art events that started to link the sculptural product to process. An example of this is a web-cast art event that I performed at the Golden Gate Jerusalem on Millennium Eve. This work showed the impossibility of representing the figurative God of Monotheism and emphasising moral forgiveness. It continued the historical narrative relation between the search for a messianic, dualistic, sculptural form and the transcendent non-duality of Eden.

This community of individuals under a higher goal was a sublimation to a Unity (within a self-other relationship) that is in contrast to the non-dual transcendental Unity of identification with the Universe. The reality of individual Forms (Platonism) is in contrast to the One Universal Form which is the mystical energy that all lower Forms emanate from (Neo-Platonism).

Computer Installations

My abstract expressionist work became more interactive, design based and linked to the Neo-Platonic transcendental unity. The dance of the drawing pen was replaced with a physical movement within an interactive sensor system space. 8 sensors were located on each side of a 365cm x 365cm frame at 30cm high. The frame was in front of a back projected screen 245cm wide and 180cm high. The whole body of the participant was involved and the subject-object distinction was broken down as the participant became intimately connected to the work that they were experiencing. The primal colours and shapes involved also related to basic instincts so as to by-pass the conscious mind.

By moving around the space the participants generated small primary coloured squares in 4 directions, within the x, y axis. The whole shape was rotated in x, z and y, z axes by another participant whilst the main participant continued to generate squares in the 4 directions. Complex forms resulted in this purely aesthetic experience. The "dance" process generated 3 dimensional forms but by-passed self-conscious ideas of form as the person moved around and experienced space in an intuitive and novel way.

The Sensor System was used as part of my artist-in-residency at Loughborough University with the C&CRS for COSTART, partly funded by the EPSRC Grant GR/M14517 Studies of Computer Support for Creative Work, Artists and Technologists in Collaboration. Mike Quantrill programmed and wrote the software for the system.

The next installation was not just an expression of the non-dual but was a deliberate and self-conscious contrast between the non-dual and the dual. It was a model of the activity of the mind in relationship to spirituality and the art forms.

Participants moved around the sensor system to build a monochrome Freudian, phallic tree of morality. This reached up to a static point, accompanied with ascending notes of music (Becoming of Being). This model showed the Western mind's search for an external, individual end Product by being active.

By being still, the group sank into a mystical sea and colourful Jungian Mandalas emerged to musical harmonies (Being of Becoming). This model showed the Eastern mind's connection to the internal Universal Process by being still. Mandalas and Hindu swastikas arose unintentionally in the mystical part of this work.

The tree symbolised life, death and morality whilst the patterns symbolised mystical eternity. This aesthetic experience of the human condition meaningfully echoed the Fall from Eden. In Jewish mystical Qabbalism Eden is interpreted as non-duality (the abstract pattern) and the Tree of the knowledge of good and evil relates to self-consciousness and duality.

2 ideas of nature are shown in this work. An abstract nature that arises immediately from the unconscious energy is symbolised as purely aesthetic design. Here the person is intimately connected to nature. A figurative representation of nature that is external to the person comes from a self-conscious subject-object relationship.

The installation also illustrates how non-dualism is the more rational perspective as it is based on experience and experimentation through meditation. In contrast the figurative faith is more about human efforts and goals. It is about faith in technology to make changes in the external world as a means of progress towards an end state.

The transition point (sinking below the sea) symbolised the link between normal consciousness and mystical consciousness. The movement between the two linked internal reality to external reality and nature to technology.

Artistic Synthesis

The main art link was in a computer project that involved an interactive performance process and a definite sculptural product. Three performances were made at Castlerigg stone circle (Cumbria, England) on Christmas day 2000, Epiphany/Orthodox Christmas day (6th January) 2001 and on the morning after the eclipse of the moon (9th January) 2001.

Expressive dance was used aesthetically but also within a meaningful event. The locations of my movements inside the stone circle (taken off footage from the video camera that I danced with) and the locations of the stones are being used to computer manufacture an AutoCAD sculpture.

The computer struts of the sculpture emanate from the location points of the stones. The sculpture is to be put on top of a virtual video installation surrounded by heads placed in the same location as the original stones. The abstract stones with a figure in the centre are transformed into figurative heads with an abstract monolith in the centre. When approaching the centre of the virtual installation gigantic struts will emanate from the head locations so that you will be within a large version of the sculpture. This serves as a temple structure and will give a sense of the sublime when you look upwards. The installation can be aesthetically appreciated but also looks at the meaning of time and faith. This work joins together nature/technology, abstract/figurative, determinism/free will, experiential/conceptual.

Conclusion

I am trying to link the human consciousness in these polarities, rather than reinforcing the split between the extremes or creating a synthesis that involves diluted versions of both. Ritual is seen as a way to link opposites. The temple housed decorative products and inside this space ritual was the process used to manifest a change. The gallery has replaced the temple and the ritual has become interactive art that makes a mystical or a moral change.

In the future I would like to combine the use of virtual spaces with ritual or temple spaces. I would like to look at the crossover point between interactive, aesthetic performance and a resulting moral product. I am currently organising a group exhibition, called The Ism (www.the-ism.co.uk), on this theme.

2. METAPHYSICAL AND ARTISTIC CREATIVITY

Energy, Form, Primal Creativity and Creation From Nothing.

The Christian tradition gives a good example of a Dualistic view of the creation of the world and the Hindu tradition gives a good example of a Non-dualistic view of creation.

The Christian view puts "being" in opposition to "nothingness" and creation comes from out of this "nothingness". The Hindu view has creation as the imposing of Form onto a pre-existent, Primal Energy/Matter and not a "Creation out of Nothing".

The two views can be linked as follows:

Non-dualistic, Primal Energy is beyond conceptual categories so it is metaphorically alluded to by the concept of "nothingness".

The dualistic Form of "Being" rather than the Form of "Nothing" is imposed onto the Primal Energy as the creative act is closer to the nature of "Being". The primal creativity instantiates the Form of "Being" and the state prior to this can be metaphorically characterised as a state of "nothingness".

Thus creation can be seen as a Hindu Forming of this Primal Energy and as a metaphorical Christian "Creation out of Nothing". Monotheism sees this "Being" as a self-created and self-conscious God. Many other contrasts remain, however, such as whether creation is a unique event or is cyclical.

Artistic Creativity

This metaphysical creativity parallels artistic creativity as non-dual creation relates to non-original, natural designs and dual creation gives rise to something from nothing.

The world is a created product and although mystics may transcend conceptual dualisms they are still situated within their created bodies. The difference is that they no longer strive for dualistic meaning. They transcend a focus on goodness but are still good by just allowing their natural goodness to show through.

Similarly design follows basic laws and principles that arise when the mind is freed from a need to create meaning. Mystical consciousness dissolves internal duality but the artist still operates in an external duality to produce design. When there is no wilful striving for dualistic meaning the innate aesthetic forms and structures arise from within the non-dual person's nature. Matter is given Form through the artist's own inner nature (non-dualistic art). Non-duality is ultimately beyond objects and is pre-creation and pre-creativity but abstract design (and process based work) is the dualistic external expression of the non-dualistic internal consciousness.

Self-conscious creativity is a dualistic activity of the free-will that shapes energy/matter. The artist wilfully Forms the Matter (dualistic art) in a meaningful expression. The dualist tries to attain an artistic or a moral product over and beyond the natural state. Moral autonomy and self consciousness allows an individual to try and reach beyond their created nature through a "freely" given inspiration, forgiveness or community action. This freedom occurs over and above karmic law, social hierarchy and tradition. Forgiveness is the perfection of moral goodness as it "creates" a goodness over and above what is required by moral law.

The Shaping Of Abstract Nature Into Figurative Nature.

The primal energy is given form as sub-atomic particles through an apparently spontaneous, random or free moment of creation out of nothing - as described in Quantum physics.

These fundamental particles are then constrained by Newtonian deterministic laws to combine as atoms and then more complex forms that eventually give rise to organisms. The organisms take on an identity independent of the constituent, abstract parts. This is similar to the way that computer abstract binary language gives rise to the phenomenon that we perceive on monitors. The complex organisms then develop a self-conscious mind that goes beyond materialistic, mechanistic, causal determinism and is free, or has the illusion of being free. The act of free will is to creatively make a choice for an element within a duality eg of good over evil.

Quantum Duality

Quantum physics gave a duality in ways of perceiving fundamental material states as either a wave or a particle. The wave is a process based field and the particle is a product based item. The quantum dualism is dissolved in a mystical non-dualism that encompasses the contrary principles by seeing them both as ultimately unreal.

Dualism relates to the Platonic Forms that shape matter and are the common features that make objects belong to a certain kind. The non-dual relates to Neo-Platonism with its Primal Form that is the source of all lesser Forms and is the mystical energy/matter. In an absolute sense these lesser Forms are unreal as everything is just a part of a universal process (the One Real Form). Non-dualism also relates to Aristotelean Nominalism which says that there are no non-material Forms outside the instances of created objects, just a shared name.

The Aristotelean Nominalism that informs contemporary metaphysical assumptions concerning matter has similarities to the Neo-Platonic/Buddhist notion and this may partly accounts for the level of acceptance that the mystical has as an aid in understanding Quantum physics. Nominalism and Neo Platonism share the materialistic view that there is no underlying reality and that all matter has an equally empty nature, with no deeper essence (Buddhist Sunyata).

Quantum Creativity

Ideal principles such as goodness are seen as illusory phenomena in extreme materialist and mystical models. I found that the reality of moral principles and free-will was directly questioned by my mystical experience. This led me to have Faith in the reality of moral truth, as well as in the reality of free choice. Whilst the correspondence of these (and other notions such as randomness) to material reality can be questioned we cannot question that we understand the terms and that they have meaning for us.

The terms morality, freedom and randomness have arisen either from a compound of other experiences or from a direct relationship to something in nature. These ideas relate to non-causality that creatively reaches beyond deterministic laws to freely make a new state. The (human or quantum) creative act gives rise to new material forms out of nothing. In contrast non-dualism is an entropy out of which no duality would have arisen without an equal and opposite (Newtonian) reaction.

This part of the Mind/Brain identity conundrum in philosophy is whether the free mind is identical to, or separate from material and causal brain states. The Platonic view puts mind (the conceptual Forms) as having the greater reality. Aristotelian Nominalism puts the material world without Forms as having the greater reality (and this perspective is associated with scientific materialism). The mystical breaks down the mind/body distinction by linking the energy underlying the material to one Universal mind. However whilst the non-dual model allows the contradictory nature of wave and particle states it does not allow a sub-atomic creation of one of the opposites from nothing as this is a dualistically free or random act beyond the material law of cause and effect.

3. THE INDIRECT BALANCING OF THE TWO CONSCIOUSNESSES IN CULTURAL HISTORY

Human beings seek a unified world paradigm and often polarise alternative perspectives. The abstract modernist perspective was rejected in postmodernism and our contemporary perspective is a relativism that says that reality is for the individual's own explanation. However the Western person is situated in a culturally relative position that informs their "immediate" response and they often fall back onto modernist assumptions for discourse on spirituality.

By looking at trends in visual culture a dynamic can be seen. The following assumes, for the sake of argument, that the mystical relates to abstract design (ie Transcendent experience) and the moral relates to figurative art (ie Gods with human attributes).

In ritual, primitive creativity linked the moral and the mystical by combining aesthetic process (e.g. meditation, music, dance and design) with meaningful products, (e.g. figures and statues). Our self-conscious need for understanding split these two perspectives and we then took them to extremes to look for a world-view.

Throughout history the psyche has subconsciously tried to re-balance these extremes in two ways. Either by balancing the spiritual with its opposite art form or by gradually moving to the opposite spiritual and art perspective (if a culture directly manifests the spiritual in art).

Cultures that saw art as secondary to the spiritual balanced views with their opposite art forms. Abstract, mystical religions balanced with figurative art forms (as in Buddhism and Hinduism). Figurative, moral religions (a God with human qualities) balanced with abstract design (as in Judaism and Islam).

The Hindu mandala is abstract as it was a direct manifestation of abstract spiritual principles, whereas Hindu figurative art is a popular embodiment of the spiritual truths.

Some cultures viewed art as equal to the spiritual and used art to directly express their views. Greek Polytheism directly manifested its figurative Gods in its art forms. Western culture inherited the Greek view of art and eventually tried to balance this figurative spirituality by moving to the abstract spirituality of Modernism.

Christianity tried to balance the figurative with the abstract by joining Greek and Jewish thinking in the doctrine of the Trinity. The Greek focus in Christianity was on the direct manifestation of the spiritual. It believed God incarnated as Jesus Christ and, in contrast, saw the Jewish view of God as non-incarnate and abstract (as the Jewish art form was abstract). The Catholics and the Orthodox focussed on this abstract God - the Father, so they balanced with figurative art and Icons. The Protestants focussed on a personal relationship with the figurative Christ, so they rejected figurative art and favoured design and simplicity.

This balancing also influenced attitudes to scientific knowledge.

The Catholic focus on an Abstract God gave rise to a need to balance with the figurative/human/technical. The Renaissance gave this balance in a Humanism that looked at the nature, philosophy and teachings of the classics. Humanists retained abstract faith in the Divine transcendence and natural order but balanced with assumptions about the importance of humanity and harnessed technology in the occult quest for the transcendent. This search also influenced the development of Jewish Qabbalism.

The Protestant focus on the figurative Jesus Christ gave rise to a need to balance with the abstract/natural. The Scientific revolution gave this balance in Natural Science. Scientists retained figurative faith in Jesus Christ but looked at God's creation, harnessing nature in the quest for the immanent truths. The art form of the time focussed on landscape and romanticism as Northern European society was moving from its figurative, dualistic position to try and encompass a more abstract natural position. Scientific modernism gradually replaced many peoples' faith with a belief in abstract mysticism and the art of abstract modernism.

The closest that people could now come to an absolute meaning was given through science and not through religion or art. Meaning in Art was seen as romantic and subjective. Semi-scientific investigations into the nature of painting looked for new, absolute meaning for art and rejected human forms in favour of abstract principles. Western culture still looked for figurative meaning and it could not accept this abstract mysticism, so in the 1960s Modernism was rejected.

Abstract and figurative, mystical and moral, were all rejected in Postmodernism. Meaning became an invalid irony. Answers were rejected but modernist and materialist assumptions remained.

Ritual was the original common point between abstract nature and figurative technology but now humanity has advanced into both extremes. We can either return to the abstract mystical or advance into the figurative technology. Rather than seeking a single answer I recognise that, ultimately, these two perspectives are separate. Mystical aesthetics provides therapeutic experiences and moral meaning brings goodness in the world. The needs for figurative meaning and to relate back to the mystical can symbolically join in our attempts to relate them through art. The best link between these positions, however, is in their shared focus on love (the mystical in identification with the universe and the moral in a community of individuals).

9 July 2001

The Opposites Linked in The-Ism

Philosophy	Primal Energy/Matter	Form
	Non-Dual	Dual
	Possible	Actual
	Virtual	Real
	Non-duality	Duality
	Transcendent	Sublime
	Mystical Experience	Moral Faith
	Internal	External
	Being of Becoming	Becoming of Being
	Jungian	Freudian
	Dionysian	Apollonian
	Feminine	Masculine
Art	Abstract	Figurative
	Continuous Process	End Product
	Aesthetic	Meaningful/Moral
	Experiential	Conceptual/Narrative
	Passive	Active
	Nature	Technology
	Immediate Nature	Representations of Nature
	(Subject=Object)	(Subject vs Object)
	Wholistic/ Universal	Atomistic/ Particular
	Collective	Individual
	Interactive Installations	Sculptural Product

Essay 2.

EAST MEETS WEST, PHILOSOPHICALLY, THROUGH ART & PERFORMANCE

This paper attempts to move away from postmodern relativism by making a map of world religions and their art forms. This map enables an analysis of underlying trends and how contradictions can be dialectically united into a dynamic relativism between two perspectives.

The visual art section is illustrated with my Game of World Religious Art and the performing art section is illustrated with my Art Religion rituals and Disco Art Religion parties.

Philosophical Method And East-West Perspectives

"Western" epistemological scepticism about the existence of objects outside our minds cannot be logically refuted, but the argument is rejected with "common sense" arguments. Postmodern relativism is scepticism over meaning and this can be rejected by showing a meaning that is "common sense". The current lack of any clear structure to an intercultural meaning reinforces the relativist's position. The Ism is an ongoing enquiry to arrange facts in a coherent structure.

In contrast my Disco Art Religion is the creation of a free space where new possibilities can arise by breaking down structure. This space is as "Club - Religion".

The Ism arose out of my own empirical spiritual enquiry, expressed through art. I chart my moral spiritual journey with a narrative, sculptural diary but this journey was interrupted when I had a mystical experience.

In the mystical experience (of "Eastern" non-duality) there was no focus on conceptual oppositions (duality). Everything was interconnected and of the same ordinary nature. Nothing was more important than anything else. There was no special meaning or meaninglessness, just an experience of being connected to the fundamental sense of reality that is the same anywhere and at anytime.

I rejected this perspective for moral reasons. It transcended good and evil and did not solve my moral conflicts, it just dissolved them as being illusory. I also rejected the experience philosophically as non-duality includes all reality, but it does not include duality, thus there is a duality between non-duality and duality. Therefore, duality is more fundamental.

However, the non-dual is still real and as a result of the experience I began a new, mystical form and method of creative work. Over time I joined this with my moral form of creativity and made an aesthetic link between the two perspectives that I couldn't make philosophically. I then saw that this model related to world spirituality and art.

The Ism took on three philosophical models. Kantian antinomies, Nietzschean views of art and Hegelian dialectic. I set up an extreme Kantian contrast (antinomies) between Western, immanent, moral dualism and Eastern, transcendent, mystical non-dualism. The art forms that relate to each perspective link to Nietzschean ideas of the Dionysian, feminine and the Apollonian, masculine.

This polarization of Eastern transcendent mysticism and Western immanent moralism is a crude stereotype of culture and art but shows an underlying structure.

The mystical relates to changing energy and process. It is non-dualistic, holistic, eternal, experiential, feminine, aesthetic and colourful. It relates to nature and natural law. It is potentiality and the primal matter of the world. It is horizontal, low cultured and domestic. The mystical breaks down the subject-object, audience-performer divisions. Abstract design and performance process are an immediate expression of this nature.

The moral relates to fixed form and to objects/products. It is dualistic, atomistic, historical, narrative, masculine, conceptual, meaningful and monochromatic. It relates to faith in technology and to free will imposing form onto nature. It is vertical, high cultured and political. The moral reinforces the subject-object, audience-performer divisions. Figurative art gives representations of this idea of nature.

I reconciled the two perspectives in a Hegelian style dialectic by joining the two art forms together. My art tries to generate an experiential link through love. Non-dual love is an identification with the universe and a dual love is between individuals in community.

Postmodern thought rejects fixed theories and emphases open possibility (as in the Disco Art Religion). I establish The Ism as a fixed model to channel this possible energy into actual form. This is like a scientific methodology, exploring possibilities to give hypotheses that are then tested against newly discovered possibilities. This hypothetical methodology is a fixed form but people remain free to reject it.

World Visual Art

The tribal self and society was united but schizophrenically fluctuated between the mystical and moral consciousnesses in animism and magic. Magic channeled mystical energy into moral forms through images. The search to understand these opposites, and for a sense of unity, led opposing cultures to develop extreme, one-sided forms of the mystical and moral models. The enlightenment individual continued in the attempt to privilege a single consciousness of the divided consciousnesses.

The Ism is an acceptance that the individual is fundamentally divided and moves between two consciousnesses. By accepting this division a limited continuity of self hood is given. This enlightened schitzophrenic fluctuates between the simultaneous need to reconcile opposites and the need to achieve a unity of one perspective over another.

I mapped the relation of mystical and moral consciousnesses to visual art and made this map into a Game of World Religious Art. This was exhibited in London in 2002 (at the Savoir Faire Art Window, New Oxford Street and at Wimbledon School of Art MA Show).

Art a) directly manifests the Divine or b) the Divine is held as being too sacred to directly manifest so is given an opposite artistic form. Given 1 (mystical abstract) and 2 (moral figurative) there are 4 possible combinations.

A1) the mystical is directly expressed in abstract art eg. Hindu mandalas or the Abstract modernism of Mondrian and Kandinsky.

A2) the moral is directly expressed in anthropomorphic art eg. Greek polytheism.

B1) the mystical is indirectly expressed in anthropomorphic art eg. Hindu and Buddhist statues.

B2) the moral is indirectly expressed in abstract art eg. Islamic and Jewish design.

Given this mapping we can see how Western culture has unconsciously attempted to synthesise the perspectives.

Applying this model we can see that Christianity is a mix of Greek (A2) and Jewish (B2) perspectives. Christianity is split between the abstract and figurative in the doctrine of the Trinity. The Greek Orthodox and the Catholics have a relationship to the more abstract God the Father, so balance with figurative icons. The Protestants have a relationship to an incarnate Son so they balance by rejecting icons, in favour of simplicity and design.

With the failure of Christianity to satisfy people in their search for meaning the abstract spirituality of the East and an aesthetic relationship to nature was looked to. Western culture adopted the Greek perspective of directly manifesting the spiritual through art.

Romanticism arose in the West and looked at nature and the sublime. The sublime experience of nature challenges our structure of reality and threatens to break it down into mystical non-duality.

Cezanne began to break down reality into the abstract, mystical field. Picasso and the Cubists tried to reconcile the split between the abstract and the figurative but Avant Garde, Communist artists like Mondrian and Kandinsky (influenced by the Eastern, mystical Theosophy) tried to create complete abstraction to directly manifest the mystical (A1). In opposition to this the Nazis (also influenced by Theosophy) rejected modern art and tried to channel (sublimate) mystical energy into a moral, figurative form (A2).

These two extremes were rejected by Western culture and a more synthetic approach was made in right wing and left wing capitalism that used Surrealism in two forms. Dadaist, Avant-Garde Surrealism was left wing and broke down everyday structures and forms into subconscious and abstract combinations. The need of art to link to the everyday was introduced when Duchamp made ordinary objects into art and art simultaneously became high-level, elite concepts and low-level, group aesthetics.

On the other hand, Dalis' classical Surrealism was right wing. It channeled abstract, subconscious energies into structured, conscious, figurative forms.

The Avant Garde had a positive and a negative role. The positive role, seen in artists like Kandinsky and Mondrian, was where structures were broken down with the idea that spontaneous, aesthetic structure might arise, in the free space created, through a connection to the mystical. The negative role, seen in Dadaism, was an operation to break down structures that the ego and super ego erect. Its efforts were seen as ongoing, needed whenever new super ego or totalitarian structures are created.

Jackson Pollock's abstract expressionist product was akin to the positive Avant Garde desire to break down structure and give spontaneous structure, however, he was a celebrity within a consumerist art structure that was used politically against Communism (and its later Stalinist, figurative, moralistic "Social

Realist" art). Rothko continued with Pollock' venture but his work marked the failure of a consumer society to be able to reach the mystical through an art commodity.

Group transcendence via commodity was then aimed at through the underground use of LSD, Op art, Psychedelic art, music, festivals and happenings (A1). This spiritual drug consumerism gave psychological casualties and highlighted a schitzophrenic relationship to culture and reality.

In contrast Andy Warhol accepted that life had become an empty, immanent commodity and reflected this in his figurative art work (A2). Rooted in a figurative (Catholic) tradition his consumer art object needed constant renewal, just like the material act of taking the Eucharist.

Warhol's empty materialism joined with the negative Avant Garde in a Postmodernism that ironically rejected consumerism, whilst remaining within it. Even meaning was a consumer spectacle to be seen in irony.

Contemporary Art And Performance

Feminist art used the body, domesticity and performance as a contrast to the masculine, Modernist institution with its abstract, gallery object. Process based happenings and environments were an Avant-Garde breaking down of male structures but the characterization of the masculine as abstract was flawed as abstract Modernism related to a feminine non-dualism, inherited from Kandinsky and Mondrian.

Warhol's plastic glamorization of the female form showed how technology harnesses the feminine energy to control feminine nature. Nature is seen as feminine and represented by the nude but man gives women the social role of sex object in order to control women's nature eg in Warhol's pop culture of making Marilyn Monroe the ultimate object. Masculine technology is seen as abstract but the spirit of the machine is faith in human endeavour. The real inner, natural, feminine principles are abstraction and design.

New feminism, however, rejects these flawed, polarised stereotypes as a masculine characterisation. It seeks a balance of masculine and feminine perspectives and art forms (A1) & (A2). Instead of nature being dominated by technology, technology is made into something natural. Techno-shamanism is a new feminist, positive Avant-Garde attempt to recreate a non-dual structure by integrating nature and technology. It is placed within a consumerist society but tries to break away from this.

Techno-shamanism is a music and a fashion but also a lifestyle. It is experiential, Dionysian and involves tribal body art, psychedelic drugs, ecstasy and trance music. It tries to synthesise completely by incorporating cyborg, robotic parts into the body.

In contrast to Techno-shamanism I use art to symbolize an end point where a link may be made between the two perspectives but do not treat this as actual. The two perspectives are symbolically linked whilst kept separate (A2) & (A1).

I accept a limited relativism between the mystical and the moral. I contrast mystical, natural aesthetic, eternal environment and performance with moral, technological, meaningful, historical art objects and concepts. I then link all of these extremes in ritual art events. The rituals can be put into domestic settings with home hologram shrine kits, and a style of clothing and music.

I use ritual in a non-drug based, technological environment, designed to mystical states of mind in order to link to energy that can be channeled into moral form. The mystics dissolve form back into energy, whereas I work to creatively channel energy. Both perspectives relate but one perspective is always in dominance.

In order to balance back with the Dionysian I also hold Disco Art Religion parties. Here music and clothing from different world religions are combined to create freedom of possibility in a free space. The manikin is used as a model to represent the controlled feminine nature of a consumerist society but in a more holistic way.

Techno-shaman artists appeal to Quantum physics to validate their views on non-duality. Quantum physics rejects that the Newtonian/Cartesian perspective is the basic reality. The Ism, however, views Newtonian consciousness is the most important way to think. Our experience of Newtonian phenomena cannot be reduced to Quantum explanations on a philosophical level.

This dualistic self-conscious is the pre-requisite for inductive progress of science. This is a historical progress that can never reach a finished project or body of knowledge. If science and mysticism really united in a non-dualistic perspective then science would freeze as there would be no need for progress in an eternal "now".

The non-dualist rejects dualistic self-consciousness as an illusion but cannot explain how this can still be a phenomenologically real experience. Non-dualism transcends the world's fixed, eternal structure to be transcended. It breaks down the mind's attempts to create fixed systems independent of this structure.

The mystic's consciousness is non-dualistically one with matter/energy. Matter and consciousness became dualistically divided with the arising of moral, self-consciousness.

Techno-shamanism moves back to mysticism and the schizophrenic, tribal self, but The Ism moves to moralism and the enlightened "schizophrenic".

Dualistic spirituality is a historical, teleological, moral and material progression. It is satisfied in the first world by nationalistic, material consumerism. Other countries know that the material end of spiritual history has not been reached and they await Messianic leaders. These Messiahs are often seen as national leaders but The Ism views everyone as an Art Messiah. It is a universal hypothesis incorporating dualism and non-dualism.

I link to a historical narrative through conceptual dialectic and empirical art enquiry. I also link to Western Monotheism by art revelations received at the Golden Gate, Jerusalem on Millennium Eve. After this event I began to use the Eastern, mystical symbol of the Swastika in rainbow form as a sign of universal Love. Thus linking mystical energy and moral narrative.

Disco Art religion allows people to explore possibilities and The Ism gives a conclusion (that remains open to growth). The two aspects to my art also show the dynamic relation between conclusion and free exploration.

25 September 2002

Mid Essays (2002-2005)

"Postmodern Religious Art"

Essay 3.

THE POSTMODERN ART WORK OF JAKE AND DINOS CHAPMAN - SITUATED WITH YOUNG BRITISH ART

Description

I found the Chapmans' "Disasters of War" are adapted toy soldiers a bit ordinary as I have had a great deal of experience in my adolescence of playing Dungeons and Dragons. The craftsmanship involved was on a par with that seen at military modelling shows just the carnage was a little more extreme. Familiarity makes the impact less strong. A sense of the sublime can be invoked by smallness as well as vastness but these works were not small or numerous enough to do either. The scale of "Hell" may produce this effect more as you wonder around the vastness and smallness and "Great Deeds Against the Dead", "Zygot" series and "Six Feet Under" work on a larger scale to create this sense.

Being both carnage and childrens' toys confuses expectation but this is nothing like the shock of seeing the Chapmans' zygotes where a real break down of expectation and categories is created. I did not know how to react to this work as it is both condemned by society (press and public) and sanctioned by society (artistic community). Our frame of reference of value is confused and appeals to authority are contradicted.

This is where their work receives its power, in destabilising both public and art spheres. However I made closure on their work by putting the interpretation of attention seekers onto them, an interpretation that links them to being selfish and right-wing. This essay looks at whether that interpretation is correct both in terms of style and content.

Nazism,Communism And Liberal Capitalism

To understand the Chapmans' work it must be put into the context of Twentieth century politics and art. In Art in Theory 1900-1990 (1) we read that abstract, avant-garde art related to communism, realism to fascism and surrealism to a blend of liberal principles and capitalist economics.

Non-dualistic, mystical theosophy was adopted by both Hitler and the Communists whilst Nazism directed its mystical energy to moral and human goals –expressed in anthropomorphic art. In contrast Communism directed its human efforts to an international unity, which the avant-garde expressed as being mystical and abstract. Communism, however, ended up like Nazism, as a Social Realism that celebrated human ideals.

Liberal Capitalism has both right and left wing Forms. Right wing art constructs anthropomorphic meaning out of the unconscious, e.g. Dali's Surrealism was anthropomorphic and linked to Franco's fascism. Left wing art deconstructs anthropomorphic meaning into abstraction, e.g. Picasso's "Guernica" turning the anthropomorphic into an abstract reaction against fascism. The Chapmans' work resembles Picasso (including details like penis style noses) but goes further. It breaks down moral systems in order to radically change the viewer's perspective.

Nazi Perspective

The Nazis built a moral structure that rejected universalism and materialism in favour of racial purity and fulfilling spiritual destiny.

In "Hitler's Vienna: A Dictator' Apprenticeship" Brigitte Hamann (2) says that Hitler saw the Hindu swastika as a mystical symbol and an Aryan "sign of the sun", and the creative force.

Hamann (3) says that Otto Weinenger's writings influenced Hitler. In "Gender and Character" he argued that the intellect and creative force was masculine and that the female principle was non-creative, degenerating and Jewish. The sexual act robbed man of his creativity and his ability to create a moral structure.

Nazi art was pastoral, romantic and local – based around German national identity. Hamann (4) says that Modern art was seen as Jewish, international and as straying from nature and returning to the primitive.

Hamann (5) says that science was also seen as Jewish, materialistic and corrupt, for example because it looked at childhood sex in Freudian psychology. There was a trend "against enlightenment and the exact sciences, and towards a new mysticism," and the Nazis preferred to direct science to serve their own ends.

Hamann (6) says that Darwin's idea of the survival of the fittest led to genetic theories and the use of eugenics to defend the Aryan race. The Nazis aimed to create a Thousand Year Reich in defence against Communism and Jewish modernism.

Communist, Avant-Garde Perspective

In contrast to this building of objective structure, the Communist Avant-Garde wanted to break down structure.

In Chapter 14 – Rabelais and His World, in "Mikhael Bakhtin", (7) Katerina Clark and Michael Holquist say that writers, like Bakhtin "reacted not so much against the bourgeoisie per se as against any kind of intellectual or moral stasis, fixity, and neatly ordered "logical" systems."

Clark & Holquist say that Bakhtin's notion of a carnival world is

"organized horizontally rather than vertically." (8) "all are considered equal and brotherhood is universal." (9) "Everything is constantly moving and changing." (10)

Carnival breaks down social oppression and

"The two principle weapons used in this onslaught by the carnival were "reverse hierarchy," which is a humbling, debunking, or debasing" "and a lowering of all forms of expression in language or art." (11)

Clark & Holquist describe how Bakhtin relates carnival to art and to language;

> "the body emphasises changes in its nature through eating, evacuation, or sex, as opposed to the static ideal represented in classical Greek marbles, is "grotesque". The grotesque body is flesh as the site of becoming." (12)

> "Life is shown in its twofold contradictory process: it is the epitome of incompleteness." (13)

Laughter, and using everyday words in language, were used to bring down authority.

Formless

The Carnival and the grotesque break down the ideal into the bodily and the horizontal and this has parallels in Bois' notion of the Formless.

"In Formless: A User's Guide" Yve-Alain Bois and Rosalind Krauss (14) give four operations of the formless; horizontality, base materialism, entropy and pulsation.

Horizontality is in the levelling of all attempts at vertical power structures like language, for example, "the article Leiris devotes to spit makes the desublimatory nature of the dictionary clear:" (15) This is part of a sabotage of academic systems, by appearing to be one whilst being incomplete and non-alphabetical.

The formless breaks down art production into its material nature.

> "the concept of image presupposes a possible distinction between form and matter, and it is this distinction, insofar as it is an abstraction, that the operation of the formless tries to collapse". (16)

Matter and form are reduced to entropy.

> "But Bataille's fascination with rot and waste, with the decomposition of everything, which finds expression in almost every one of his texts, shows well enough that the entropic freeze, whether or not he wanted to keep it at bay in his writing, was an essential operation for him, all the more violent in that it was inevitable and its effectiveness depended on no one's will." (17)

A basic energy is left. This pulsation echoes the sexual and gives a bodily emphasis. It breaks down the idealised as it "involves an endless beat that punctures the disembodied self-closure of pure visuality and incites an irruption of the carnal." (18) We cannot just coldly observe the carnal, we are enticed to become involved in it.

This sexual materialism is a feature that the Nazis sought to avoid.

Young British Artists

In order to understand the Chapmans' work it is useful to relate it to the work of other Young British Artists who give a complex mix of both right and left wing concerns.

In "High Art Lite" Stallabras sees the YBA's as rejecting the deep psychology and metaphysics of traditional modern art (19) and as seeing social responsibility and moral sense as no longer ideologically possible (20).

In their place the YBAs give us crude visual pleasures that cause liberalist moral objections (21) and conceptual one-liners that make an immediate impact (22). They return to anthropomorphic concerns but their work confronts the viewer with the abject, it is liminal (between states) and it destabilizes fixed meaning. The work never makes closure and this allows it to be more than subjective whilst remaining purely subjective. The work is not further justified or explained because the work has an anti-theoretical base and is autonomous of theory.

Criticism Of YBA

On (23) Stallabras notes how American critic Alexandra Anderson-Spiby viewed "Sensation" as a lesser imitation of earlier work by international artists. Stallabras goes on to say (24) that American critics David Frankel and Robert Storr dislike the YBA art for being local, naïve and parodic. This original combination (of international style and provincial content), however, is seen as a strength by Roberts in "Domestic Squabbles".

On (25) Stallabras says that many YBAs glorify the urban as the pastoral once was glorified. The proletariat is seen as the natural (non-conceptual) worker but when the artist takes on the role of being this worker then they cannot give a theoretical meaning to their work without destroying this naturalist stance. Yet he thinks that they do have a stance. A relation to Nazi glorification of the pastoral is possible here and on p271 Stallabras notes that the demise of the Avant-garde left no single, clear political stance and that the ideals of post modern orthodoxy have fallen to consumer atomism. YBAs gives complicity to this by not making statements against it. This point is emphasized by Ralph Rugoff, Fop Art in "www.LAweekly.com" who says that the audience of the YBA work is very conservative (including, in 1997, the Tory Heritage Secretary), despite its neo-liberal posturing.

This conservatism is passed off as socialism as on (27) Stallabras says that the YBAs have an oceanic oneness with everything, that fits with new labour as art is joined to the working class in a classless class, but it is particular that pretends to be universal. I think that this shows YBA wants to link back to anthropomorphic meaning but needs to distance itself from fascism idealistic art forms. As a result the YBAs glorify the abject but Stallabras, however, notes earlier how the YBAs are patronizing to the working class by seeing them as dirty, violent and sex focussed.

John Roberts, in "Domestic Squabbles" (28) says that whilst the YBA work reduced the possibility of historical and critical debate as a source material for art it also expanded the possibilities for art to go outside the academy and to include the everyday. But in putting high culture and low culture in opposition Stallabras (29) says that extreme reactions from both camps were created, and not a suspension of judgement as intended. The display of Marcus Harvey's Myra in the "Sensation" exhibition is used as an example of this, where the press went into 2 opposing camps at the painting of Hindley made out of childrens' handprints.

On (30) HAL Stallabrass thinks there is a contradiction as the YBA world is fragmented but so much is made of the artists personality (On p43 he says Tracey Emin was seen as authentic, primitive and spiritual in her honesty. Emin has self as the work and for Damien Hirst the self is the celebrity.)

On (31) Stallabras notes another contradiction. Whilst the YBAs reject moral statements they also seek admiration for their honesty. I think that this honesty is a minimum condition for progress in art and the work of the Chapmans is an attempt to be brutally honest and Matthew Collings says "Their trick, which so far has been completely effective, is to make all this seem very tied to real problems of modern life". In contrast to the YBAs, however, the Chapmans also articulate a clear theory and purpose to their work.

How The Chapmans Are Distinct

Most YBAs reject explicit theory but the Chapmans directly state it.

The work of the YBAs links to the Nazis in their glorification of the local and the national but also links to Bakhtin's Carnival and the Formless. The Chapmans move away from nationalism and are more international.

The YBAs set up oppositions that they do not break down completely but the Chapmans aim to completely break these down.

Their work is more radically anti capitalist, breaking down male, dominatory, conceptual structure. In their interview with Douglas Foght, (32) the Chapmans say that their work is "dramatically anti conception. We always claim that it doesn't pertain to any kind of meaning. If anything, it pertains to an attack on conscious meaning, which we see conceptual art as constantly prioritizing". They go on to state that their work is non-political because it is scatological and tries to break down culture by rejecting language and structures of power. To do this they seek a libidinal discharge that is not representational but is iconic, directly relating to the unconscious.

In their interview with Maia Damianovic (33) the Chapmans say how they are breaking down the "self". They are against singularities, the notion of an autonomous self, humanism and the notion of God. They go on to say that want to create a kind of convulsion between oppositions that relates to the Kantian notion of the Sublime and produces a cultural value of nil. This convulsion between oppositions also relates to the breaking down of a sense of interior and exterior between individuals.

In Artforum Jan Avgikos (34) says that the Chapmans' postmodern precursors keep an interest in subjects (or the artist) whereas the Chapmans deny subject-hood and see themselves as one with culture and as post-art. However, also in Artforum, Rachel Witherrs (35) asks that if the Chapmans are one with culture then how can they criticize it?

This working within culture is further described by Mark Sladen in Art Monthly (36). As a reaction to fragmentation, the body has been used by contemporary artists to have the appearance of being an "authentic" expression. The unified body can be used as a reaction to fragmentation or as a way to use fragments, fetishes or traces to reclaim the body from technological fragmentation. The best body art does not see these fragments as mythic, nor does it try to look at the body from a stance outside of culture. The Chapmans look at the body from within culture and how identity is formed through childhood in fashion and pornography. I think that the Chapmans celebrate the breakdown of identity and they think that entropy is an inevitable reaction to attempts to form identity.

This inclusion in culture marks how the Chapmans reject a pastoral perspective. In "Gender is an Organic Superstition" (37) the Chapmans explain that they think that sexual difference arises from out of our sense of having a separate ego. This binary division is part of the nature of capitalist thinking, with reproduction occurring on both industrial and organic levels. He rejects the idea of Mother earth as it is just a contrary binary so he seeks to transgress that split of nature and technology via genetics. The hybrid forms are iconic of our inner selves and part of the shock is in seeing ourselves reflected.

That an entropy and unescapable materiality of the world remains is pointed to in Unholy Libel, Gagosian Gallery 1997, Revelations: A conversation between Robert Rosenblum and Dinos & Jake Chapman. Here (38) the Chapmans said that;

"Goya's Great Deeds Against The Dead represent, as we see it, a Humanist crucifixion. "Humanist" because the body is elaborated as flesh, as matter. No longer the religious body, no longer redeemed by God. Goya introduces finality – the absolute terror of material termination."

Our own materiality is referred to again in Unholy Libel, "We are interested in them (mannequins) because they preexist. And if they preexist materially they preexist conceptually, and in that sense they represent the embodiment of a certain form of desire." (39) These embodiments are then arranged in endless permutations.

Unholy Libel, Rosenblum sees a parallel to Sol Le Witt in their endless permutations of and combinations of simple geometric vocabularies – but substituting human biology for the geometries breaks down the body and form. The Chapmans describe how;

"We are particularly interested in Sol Le Witt and Carl Andre. Specifically in the construction of complex languages which occur as dysfunctional systems" "without the semblance of communication." (40)

This breakdown in language (and conflation of opposites) paralyses the rational mind and the noumenal, unconscious energy appears. The breakdown allows the noumenal to appear and the viewer can react in 2 ways.

In Doctorin' the Retardis (in Chapmanworld) David Falconer (41) says that "in his introduction to 'The Postmodern Condition', Lyotard traces the postmodern 'split' in the difference between an affirmative and a reactive response to modern art's devotion to the sublime aesthetic." The affirmative enjoys the dissolution of values and the reactive tries to find a fixed truth when faced with that dissolution of values. For the affirmative "irony registers an allegience to the failure of presentation". (42)

Falconer says that Loe Bersani states that the sublime is a rush of libidinal energy caused when presentation utterly fails. Lyotard's affimative person enjoys this failure and slides into the "noumenal swamp of the body" (43). The self no longer differentiates itself from the world in an ecstatic "spiral beyond cognition" (44).

Douglas Fogle's article later in Chapmanworld (45) also relates to this paroxysm to induce a sense of the transcendent. He describes work of the Chapmans where the Romantic theology of the artist is replaced with a more scatological (the science of filth) notion of the sacred. He quotes the Chapmans "When our sculptures work they achieve the position of reducing the viewer to a state of moral panic... they're completely troublesome objects." (46)

Falconer (47) says that Bersani describes Freud as unable to frame proper conduct as his debate always moves into the area of perversion and his text contains incoherence and self contradiction. Psychoanalysis is thus unable to make closure, ie to give definite answers.

In "Art in America" Eleanor Haertney (48) sees "Six Feet Under" is seen as a kind of expulsion from Paradise. I think this fits with Jewish mystical Qabbalists who associate Eden with a state of non-duality, prior to the Fall. Although the Chapmans never explicitly state that they seek to make a link to the mystical the duality arises via concepts and it is these concepts that the Chapmans are trying to suspend..

Conclusion

A number of essays see how the Chapmans make reference to art history but are nonetheless just fashionable and ineffective. In Flash 186, Martyin Maloney (49) thinks the Chapmans' work is like Bakhtin, in finding beauty in the grotesque. However their work is second-rate art with a pretence to being something grander, profound and endurable. Too dull to engage people, the art equivalent of Bros, appropriating meanings but soon to be forgotten. Stallabras (50) thinks they do not provoke the desired reaction of moral panic but only one of laughter at their oddly familiar objects, streamlined to fit the mass media.

Some critics think that their work is ill-formed. In "New Art Examiner" Martha Schwendener (51) thinks that "Six Feet Under" refers to Nazi concentration camps and also rejects the sacred boundaries of the body. "The penises, button holes and labia stuck on the figures are repulsive (like the celebrated big toe of Bataille's essay on the Informe) and yet sexually charged. It is a matter of arrangement and disarrangement. But, as in both Bataille and Deleuge and Gualtari, there is never a logical version of how things should be". She continues that "The Chapmans, obsessed with their own bad-boy aura, have cobbled together, in both their objects and their writings, a hodgepodge of theory that reeks of trendiness." (52)

Neal Brown in Art & Text (53) recognises that the Chapmans have a clear purpose in Great Deeds Against the Dead but thinks its references to Christianity and its imagery and painting technique (of blood on clean skin) confuses spiritual meaning with sexual pleasure and in seeking outward psychic change it is involuted and ultimately self-extinguishing.

Charges of Fascism

Stallabras (54) thinks the Chapmans present as critique against liberal ideals and morals but come from the right as they enslave the viewer into reaction that induces moral panic and that is anti-idealistic. Stallabras (55) notes how Gilbert and George appeal to right wing tastes and interests. They are interested in people, conservatism and are anti-theoretical. Dinos Chapman worked for

Gilbert and George and was influenced by their work. However, as I have shown, this anti-idealism is intended to be anti-fascist.

Stallabras also notes (56) that in a controversial essay published in the Modern Review and then the Guardian, Julie Burchill criticized Jake Chapman as being fascist because he thought entry to the gallery should depend on whether you had sufficient education. In Unholy Libel the Chapmans state that they aim at a bourgeois audience:

"We are interested in recuperating every form of terrorism in order to offer the viewer the pleasure of a certain kind of horror, a certain kind of bourgeois convulsion – everybody else visits theme parks." (57)

It is not clear if they aim at a bourgeois audience to manipulate them or whether they are just opportunists that are complicit with capitalism and fascism. In Life: the Observer Magazine, Lynn Barber (58) says that Saatchi couldn't get enough of them. Jake boasted at the time, "Manipulating art people is like galling off a log." Dinos added, "We feel sorry for our friends who don't understand the game."

In "Sulpture" Laurie Attias (59) The Chapmans' zygotic work resemble Nazi genetic experiments on children, as well as mirroring "the sculpted bodies of "official" Nazi sculptor Arno Breker and propaganda art of the 1930s". But I think that instead of these being ideal constructs they attempt to break down conscious thinking. The perfect classical forms of fascism are replaced with perfect consumer forms of capitalism, but these are broken down in an Avant-Garde venture. The work is more honest than that of other YBAs as it shows human nature but also does not pretend to be outside of the consumerist gallery and elitist art structures.

Problems with Chapmans Theory

Even though Stallabras (60) quotes Jake Chapman as saying that "If the work didn't work then we'd need to say what it all means" the Chapmans work contains a great deal of theory. Stallabras says (61) that YBA work doesn't need a theory, and contradicts current theoretical frameworks because it is theoretically neutral. To criticize it a new theoretical framework is needed. I think, however, that the Chapmans articulated their relation to the old theoretical framework.

Stallabras says (62) that the Chapmans' use of theory is in a slightly self-mocking tone eg in its references to Dr Who. One reason for not taking themselves seriously may be due to a moral criticism of their work.

In "Frieze" Jonathan Jones (63) on the Disasters of War at the White Cube says
"The cinematic representations of the Holocaust that everyone in the West has by now experienced have done nothing to prevent a new catastrophe in Kosovo. If modern history has taught us one thing it's that we can aestheticise any horror."

This moral reading misses the point of trying to break down moral and intellectual structures in order to achieve a different perspective. However it is on the moral level that the majority of people will always operate and as such their work is elitist. The Chapmans laughingly play into attention seeking but also have a serious point.

13 March 2002

Essay 4.

IS ARTAUD'S INCLUSIVE THEATRE REALLY EXCLUSIVE?

In "Artaud's Theatre of Cruelty" Albert Bermel states that one of Artaud's 5 theatrical innovations is to encompass the audience within the performance. This inclusion of the audience, however, is seen as problematic by Iris Marion Young.

I wish to relate this innovation to another contemporary question concerning Anton Artaud and the "Theatre of Cruelty" and this question must be dealt with first as it is what is the theoretical framework that led Artaud to want to include the audience.

The framework comes from Artaud's Gnostic conception of the universe, as described by Jane Goodall in "Artaud and the Gnostic Drama". Goodall argues that Artaud was influenced by the Gnostic idea of God as demi-urge who imposes a masculine order onto feminine matter. In Artaud's second letter of his "Letters of Cruelty" we read how he considers the world to be naturally evil and that the creation of goodness has to be desired and willed. This creative action, however, creates more evil despite the will for creating goodness. (1)

I think that this seeming paradox can be explained by two conceptions of goodness, an immanent goodness and a transcendent goodness. For Artaud the Gnostic's world is immanent and fallen. As a result all created goodness is just part of a fallen nature and cannot be truly good. True goodness is achieved only in transcending the immanent world. This characterisation of Artaud's position is evidenced in his article entitled "An Affective Athleticism". Here he posits that inhaling is a masculine, creative act and exhaling is a feminine dying. We achieve a balance between the two in a sacred breathing, overcoming and balancing, these opposites. This breathing overcomes the cycle of opposites of life an death in a transcendent (seventh breath) state.

"And a seventh state higher than breathing, uniting the revealed and the unrevealed through the portals of a higher Guna, the state of Sattva." (2)

The "Sattva" is beyond opposites (dualities) and is non-dual. This non-dualistic (encompassing) nature of Artaud's "Theatre of Cruelty" is problematic for Iris Marion Young as she thinks that any community created also creates a new duality between those within and those excluded from the community. Must the Theatre of Cruelty transcend this if it is to be successful and if so then how does Artaud overcome this problem?

Gnostic Drama

Goodall contrast Nietzsche's and Artuad's views of God to show how the Gnostic viewpoint differs from a traditional Western perspective.

For Nietzsche and Artaud God enslaves us through language (3). For Nietzsche the release from God's or language's control is through Dionysian dance and music. For Artaud release is through "total theatre".

In Chapter 7 Goodall describes Nietzsche as leaving rational structures in place whilst Artaud breaks these down. Artaud calls us to throw off this God who leads us only into matter and away from our true self. The self needs reconstructing by violently rejecting the Laws of God (4).

The Nietzschean rejection of God is not like Artaud's rejection. Nietzsche's God is impotent and does not have a full degree of feelings. Artaud's God has feelings but Artaud calls us to throw off this God who leads us only into matter and away from our true self. The self needs reconstructing by violently rejecting the Laws of God (5).

Nietzsche's God is philosophical, he is the enemy because he is a phantasm that stops men asking authentic questions for themselves. In contrast Artaud sees the first crime as coming much earlier than this, it arises with ontology and the questions themselves need rejecting. Language creates the notion of a self and the thought of "I" causes the real self to disappear.

The original cosmic presence is stolen and cannot be regained (prior to language). Artaud rejects God's purloining of presence through creating radical difference in his theatre in order to show the dualisms that need transcending. In Artaud's Gnostic drama cruelty meets cruelty. Artaud is not just against language but against the body and the created world itself.

Goodall asks whether Nietzsche or Artaud destroy Western metaphysics most decisively. For Nietzsche destiny belongs to the individual, rather than God, but Nietzsche still uses a Western philosophical system, based on language, dialectic and conceptual oppositions. In contrast Artaud engages both in a theoretical and a practical (dramaturgical) way. His Theatre threatens theology and spoken language (logos).

Artaud is not seeking an endpoint that mankind aims for and he does not posit an origination point. Goodall (6) quotes Derrida's *Writing and Difference*,183 saying that Artaud's art is without works. This is because Artaud is fighting against the notion of a creator God/demi-urge

> "by crediting him with an art without works. Derrida refuses Artaud the status of creator, which is his most complex, persistent, and impassioned claim against the demiurgical imposition of constituted being."

She also says Foucault describes Artaud as giving a madness that emphasises the presence of an absence, or a void of works.

Goodall, however, quotes Artaud as saying that

> "My work represents a battle with *god* and Satan in which I have not yet gained the victory, a war of usury which nevertheless is approaching its end.(xxv.109)" (7)

"Artaud equates creation with cruelty and proposes to undertake the work of counter-cruelty in his theatre".

Goodall says (8) that Susan Sontag says that Gnosticism is the attempt to free the spirit from a world where matter is vile and the spirit is in conflict with the body and all its instincts. Sontag criticises Gnosticism as an "Exacerbation of dualisms", between inner and outer space and between individual and socio political concerns. For Sontag this criticism is then applied to Artuad. Artuad's theatrical revolution cannot occur because it does not create a political revolution, only a personal one.

Goodall says that Sontag's requirement of total revolution misses the process based nature of Gnosticism. Sontag is seen as mistaken because for her:

"The dynamic idea of gnosis is replaced by a terminal prognosis; highly charged oppositions are defused in a vision of extreme solipsism; a catalytic experience of alienation is exchanged for a condition of alienation that is stagnant."

By making the Gnostic view static it rejects the idea of continued attempts to transcend dualities in order to reach a Gnostic perspective. I do not think that this counters Sontag's criticism because a partial or an ongoing revolution can still be solipsistic unless the catalytic experience also diffuses the opposites of political and solipsistic.

This gives a similar question of whether Gnostic theatre includes the opposites of audience and performer. Does it include the audience in a breaking down of dualities, as by creating a "non-dual" space a new exclusivity is created. It is this exclusivity that is criticised in Artaud's model of inclusive theatre.

Exclusion in Community

Baker-White says (9) that Philip Austalander differentiates 2 strains of Holy Theatre, the communal and the individual. Catharsis can occur on an individual as well as on a communal level. Austlander puts Artaud on the individualist side of the split between individual and collectivist .

Baker-White does not think that this does justice to Artaud. "The Theatre and its Double" (trans. Mary Caroline Richards New York: Grove Press 1958) gives two types of Artaudian community. Communities of signification are where expressions and images are the same and people "receive signals of the Theatre of Cruelty on the same wavelength and to the same effect. "Communities of knowledge" (whether hidden or explicit) where certain secret truths are expressed objectively. These truths to be experienced directly and immediately. This is achieved through mass spectacle and the agitation of the masses.

> "Practically speaking, we want to bring back the idea of total theatre, where theatre will recapture from cinema, music-hall, the circus and life itself, those things that always belonged to it." (10)

Although for Artaud these forms of community remain hidden behind conventional theatrical representation (11, the hope was to recover community through the denial of representation and other artistic mediating agencies (most specifically texts).

Artaud saw theatre as illusory and divisive, but he also saw life as illusory and divisive.

> "What could prevent me believing in the illusion of theatre since I believe in the illusion of reality?" (12).

By going beyond representation, Artaud hoped to go beyond everyday life. He used traditional, referential techniques to "cruelly" question the beliefs and expectations of the audience. He simultaneously used repetition and a tight script as a form of mantra or koan. Meditational breathing and actions involve the experience of the audience and connect them to a deeper reality.

> "The show will be coded from start to finish, like a language." (13)

> "This ghostly soul can be regarded as exhilarated by its own cries, otherwise what are the Hindu mantras, those consonances, those strange stresses where the soul's secret

side is hounded down into innermost lairs, to reveal its secrets publicly." (14)

"We must allow the audiences to identify with the show by breath and beat by beat." (15)

"The key to throwing the audience into a magical trance is to know in advance what pressure points must be affected in the body." (16)

Baker-White says that Young sees a flaw in positing a "true" "presence" in the communitarian moment where the subjects are no longer exterior to one another (17). The "Theatre of Cruelty" goes beyond conflict and violence to an exclusionary unity that gives an image of non-exclusionary mutuality, devoid of conflict and violence. Baker-White suggests that the "work was both enlivened and plagued by the paradox of the Artaudian legacy" (18). Baker-White says that Derrida recognises the paradoxical impossibility of Artaud's task.

Derrida thinks the "Theatre of Cruelty" inhabited, rather than produced, non-theological space, free from the mediated process of representation and the model of this was communal festival (19). Derrida saw Artaud wanted to reject repetition, duality and representation. He wanted to break down difference in order to reach a pure presence. This was done by rejecting "text, spatial segmentation, historical referentiality and even the division between actor and role". It think this view does not account for Artaud's continued use of all these conventions in a bodily way, in order to transcend them.

In the "First Manifesto" of "The Theatre of Cruelty" Artaud does "not mean to bore the audience to death with transcendental cosmic preoccupations" (20), although these must be there. He also does

"not intend to do away with dialogue, but to give words something of the significance that they have in dreams." (21)

This suggests that his choice of plays, disregarding their text (eg. Shakespeare, Elizabethan theatre works, Buchner's Woyzeck (22)), still have a concern to include and entertain the audience e. however the concern is also to break down their conscious understanding and allow their unconscious understanding to operate by way of the mantric rhythms of the plays.

Baker-White introduces Young who gives a number of criticisms of community that can relate to Artaud's Theatre (223). I think 4 of these are important.

She says 1) that an oppositional ways of thinking (like community and difference characterised as feminine and masculine respectively) is part of bourgeoise culture and cannot be reversed to get outside of that culture by reversing roles, e.g. women acting with masculine characteristics. This reversal just reinforces masculine, oppositional ways of thinking. This implies that the world's cruelty cannot be overcome with Artuad's counter cruelty.

Young also thinks 2) the oppositional way of thinking also contains the problematic notion of a concrete Cartesian individual self within a community (24). She goes on to say that Julia Kristeva (Kristevca, "Le sujet en process," "L'experience et la pratique," "Matiere, sense, dialectique," *Polylogue* –pp.55-136, 263-86) sees the self as divided (conscious and unconscious) and unable to show itself fully to society or even to itself. This suggests that a full community is an impossible ideal as the members cannot show themselves fully. The oppositional other is hidden from view in order for the self to maintain a false appearance of integrity.

Young further thinks 3) that the desire for an exclusive unity at the expense of valuing diversity has the same underlying motives as the desires for racism (25).

Young also feels 4) that positing an idea of an established Utopian community in opposition to a current society sets up oppositions between the present and the future and is not helpful in creating social change.

Artaud's "Theatre of Cruelty" can overcome all 4 of Young's objections as follows:

1) It removes bourgeois oppositional thought in favour of experience.

2) It shows a true, whole self and not an illusory, divided self.

3) It breaks down all desires of exclusivity in an open, theatrical experience.

4) It is part of an ongoing theatrical, meditative process of change.

Baker-White applies Young's ideas of a divided, bourgeois "self" (seeking to establish an ideal vision through community) to Artuad's theatre. This, however, does not take into account Artaud's notion of the cruelty of a sudden rupture to achieve a changed state of consciousness, continually renewing itself and thus also bringing about a social change.

In contrast Young appeals to the idea of a heterogeneous society in a communitarian unity that explores difference but the Artaudian, Gnositic community goes beyond this unity made of different parts. Its unity is in the source that all division and unity originate from. This position is beyond philosophical reason. Artuad's "work is a rejection of the philosophical and a rejection of "work" – within a world created by a "philosophical", logos based Demiurge.

Using Young to describe Artaud's model does not allow for Artaud's solution, the acceptance of contradiction to paralyse rationality and thus transcend contradiction. However an adapted version of Young's point can be made as if the philosophical reason is rejected there still remains a duality (or exclusion) between experiential non-duality (for transcendence) and philosophical duality (or inclusion/exclusion).

Artaud seeks to transcend the notions of community and individuality so that individuals can realise that they, the performers and the audience, are identical to the essence of the universe. This view explains why Artaud could be interpreted by Auslander and Sontag as individualistic and by Baker-White as communitarian.

Maintaining the difference between spectator and performer shows the impossibility of the theatre to create full community. Artaud was aware of this problem and was also very conscious that any high metaphysics would alienate his audience and would not achieve the transcendent effect that he sought. He realised that he needed a narrative basis to maintain the attention of the audience but used cruelty to remove dependence on this narrative so that a deeper sense of transcendence would be achieved through breathing techniques.

Contemporary Examples

A number of works by 60's and 70's artists using Artaudian themes are described by Baker-White as relating to this issue of community and Young's objections to it. I will look at The Open Theatre's "The Serpent" as it relates to Eden, the Fall and ideas of God. These are all important to an understanding of Gnosticism and thus of Artaud's theatrical goal.

Joseph Chaikin's Open Theatre was committed to process, presence and change. Their most renowned production, "The Serpent" began as a series of exploratory exercises in 1967. Based on the book of Genesis but including both mythological and historical events "The Serpent" drew on the energies and inspiration of ritual and community based interaction. The actors were like priests doing the questioning for the congregation. Chaikin "hoped to discover forms that would express both the deepest, most private areas of experience and the external, public experience that communities share". (Blumenthal, *Joseph Chaikin* 118).

The actors took on various roles in a process of instantaneous and open character transformation. In Eden they were "birds, beasts, plants forms and amorphous pulsating things" (26). Eventually two actors differentiated themselves as Adam and Eve. The rest become the Serpent. After Adam bit the apple God confronted Adam and Eve and was seen as a kind of possession between them. No single character was God, he spoke through various actors. "Community through pure presence reaches here beyond the bonds of the living into the fictional space of otherworldliness." (27) On Baker-White says that Blumenthal (op cit 118) notes how after eating the apple a senses of difference and separation grew. The paradox of Artaud's theatre and representation reappeared. Baker-White coincidentally notes how the Utopian community of the Open Theatre itself became more fractured as the production and company developed over time.

Baker-White concludes that "the organic concept is never complete because the audience is always caught in a space between the authenticity of presence and the theatrical act of representation." (28). thus community is not satisfied. He gives an example where the Performance Group presented Akropolis (approximately 1962) (Schechner, Performance Theory, 83) and a member of the audience repeatedly disrupted a performance, took possession of a prop gun and started an argument with cast members that almost became a fist fight. He sees this as possible evidence that the impossibility of pure community of presence within the medium of theatre causes rupture that allows the Artaudian call for violence to manifest itself in the performative moment involving the spectator.

I think that the violence is in the impossibility of being able to transcend the world completely. Artuad showed the impossibility in a paradox/paralysis. Artuad does not seek to create a community, he seeks to transcend notions of community and individuality so that individuals can realise that they, the performers and audience are identical to the essence of the universe. This view explains why Artaud was seen, by Austlander and Sontag, as individualistic and, by Baker-White, as communitarianism.

I think that maintaining the difference between spectator and performer allows the impossibility of Artaud's works and this paralyses the rational mind and belief in the ability of the theatre to achieve its effects. This facilitates a violent rupture in the spectator that displaces thought and allows experience to take over, with a possible transcendent effect. Thus Artaud's theatre can be seen as going beyond classifications such as inclusive and exclusive.

A more contemporary example was "The Singularity". A play performed at the Camden People's Theatre by "Foolish People" on Saturday 14th September 2002. The main protagonists were Dr Ruth Bell, a pantheist and scientist and Rebecca Beelz, a Christian evangelist. The play involved a confusing mixture of roles in a fictional scene from the destruction of reality by the gravitational influence of a black hole. This gravity fluctuation was seen as bringing about a new creation and the appearance of a messiah/devil figure who was also the reincarnation of Dr Bell's murdered baby son.

The Christian attempts to rationalise the singularity as God's new creation (claiming that the last singularity coincided with the Biblical dating of creation) and the scientist rationalises this away. We find that in reality the fluctuation brings about a cruel Karmic balancing of the protagonist's deeds. There is no divine love in the play. Even the messiah figure is seen as a devil figure before finally being revealed as Dr Bell's murdered son. This Karmic balancing is the modern equivalent of the Godless natural law of the Plague, seen as a redeeming epidemic by Artaud in "Theatre and the Plague" (29) as it destroys all, regardless of their status.

In the FoolishPeople website we find a description of the performance:

> "The Singularity marks the continuation of FoolishPeople's work on interactive live art. FoolishPeople continue to pioneer theatre where performers engage and interact with audience members in an immersive and real environment. This creates a unique and personal journey for each audience member.
>
> Through reactive and interactive environments FoolishPeople will lead the audience of the singularity through the failure of reality to the ultimate truth." (30)

This ultimate truth is related to an Artaudian, Gnostic non-duality and the break down of audience/performer distinctions was part of the strategy to reach this.

Prior to the show the audience sat in the theatre café. Here information was displayed, purporting to be for a scientific conference on the gravitational singularity. Some of the actors pretended to be theatre goers and I was asked by a strangely clad actor to pass on the message that "Your mother wants you to know that she loves you" to a member of the actor audience. Passing this message on I was greeted with the response, "My mother is dead".

I did not know hat the other person was an actress so this surprised me and made me feel guilty about upsetting them. I became uneasy about my surroundings and was unclear as to how cruel the play would be towards my self and its audience. I also wondered who was really apart of the audience or a part of the play.

When the audience was asked to go to the main theatre via the street an actress gestured wildly from the theatre window we passed. We met her in the theatre when she appeared from the window space. Halfway through the one hour and ten minutes performance the audience was asked to move between the theatre and the café area. The aim was to make us feel as if we were at a real conference and that a real event was taking place. This further broke down our sense of what was real and what was fiction.

The stage space was intimate, designed as a hotel bedroom with adjoining bathroom (offstage left). Violent murders took place in the bathroom. Blank ammunition was fired on the main stage and the male actor appeared naked as a grown up baby son carrying real animal entrails (supposedly of his murdered father) onstage and draping them onto his mother. Incestuous murdering of wife, husband, child and parent were staged as were supernatural sex scenes. All of these factors increased the level of shock and cruelty in the performance.

The play successfully made me wonder what would happen to me in the theatre. It produced a sense of unease as to where the violence would end and whether any would be inflicted upon my self. The noise of the gun-fire and the screaming made me physically uncomfortable but the narrative of the cast became implausible. When I became unconvinced then the violent acts became spectacle and not something affecting me personally. Although they may have exposed primal instincts these were not responded to in the barrage of unbelievable, supernatural events. The cruelty ceased to be realistic and became repetitive and predictable.

Artaud's method is to expose your emotions and feeling as being corrupt and to shock you into seeing the fallen nature of your system of thought of and desire. "The Singularity" achieved this and I was reminded what a corrupt and cosmically meaningless place the universe might be, yet this very acceptance gave me a vantage point.

The play reflected Artaud's Gnostic ideas in its view of the created world as barbaric and corrupt. A singularity is a breath-like fluctuation of creation and void. Karma plays a dominant role, with a strong sense of judgment levelling out good and evil, and in the denying of the evangelist's perspective and her eventual exposure, judgment and punishment for being a hypocrite and murderer.

The rhythmic and repetitive nature of "The Singularity" contrasted with its seeming spontaneity in a cosmic inevitability. The ending of the play, however, was melodramatic and not rhythmic breathing mantra. Although the plot was deliberately convoluted there was still too much of a narrative resolution to focus on. Maybe this reflected the impossibility of transcendence, whilst still emphasising the need for it and creating a space where a breakdown of traditional thinking allows for the possibility of experiencing it.

On the FoolishPeople website an article called "Technotopia & the death of Nature", by James John Bell, describing the idea of the singularity.

> "A number of respected scientists and futurists now are predicting that technological progress is driving the world towards a "Singularity" – a point at which technology and nature will have become one. At this juncture, the world as we have known it will have gone extinct and new definitions of "life", "nature" and "human" will take hold." (31)

The play conflates the notion of uniting opposites with the notion of a black-hole singularity and a fluctuation in space and time, bringing about a change in consciousness. There is little in the play to suggest the meeting of machines with humanity and nature. The singularity here is more a levelling of all creation with its opposite so as to create a free space, but emphasising the barbarity of the situation and suggesting a need to transcend this.

In response to Young's 4th criticism (of the exclusivity of an Artaudian theatre) we see that "The Singularity" breaks down masculine oppositional ways of thinking into their opposites. The protagonists are female and their roles change between sexes as they are reincarnations of various people. This breaks down the sense of an individual identity and emphasises a sense of the futility of identity and the arbitrariness of it. It does not posit an ideal way to be for society to aim at, rather, it rejects social systems and seeks to transcend them.

Despite attempts to integrate with the audience I still felt very distant from the action and the performers. I did not feel that they were creating a sense of community through the work and they did not want to talk with the audience after the performance, which I had hoped to do.

"The Singularity" has a number of the outward conventions and theoretical interests of Artaud's "Theatre of Cruelty" but it fails to generate the intensity of experiences that make a link to the deeper community of knowledge, where knowledge relates to the specialised meaning of the Greek word, Gnosis.

1 June 2002

Essay 5.

THE ART AND PERFORMANCE OF ANTHONY PADGETT

In this essay I look at the autobiographical and philosophical underpinnings at the beginning of the mid-career artistic practice of myself, Anthony Padgett. I then examine how these affect my visual and performance practice. I present the objectives and the different artistic methods I employed to achieve these objectives (including exhibitions of sculptures and performances, using mixed media, in clubs). I then contrast these methods with those of other artists.

Objectives

The general objective of my work is to find an authentic art that expresses the question of whether there is any divine reality and if this reality might have a practical function.

A specific objective of my work arose out of a revelation I received at the Quaker Meeting House, St. Martins Lane, London, in 1994. I was in London working on historic churches, teaching religious education and doing interfaith work. I sat in a meeting and the instant that I questioned whether we need religious buildings, there was thunder and lightning directly over the meeting house. I came out of the meeting and saw a book lying on the table about the reconstruction of Jerusalem, by the modern architect Moshe Safdie.

I felt that Jerusalem was the centre of religious conflict and that the book was a sign to go there to find if religious art has any real value. I left through the adjoining Quaker Art Gallery and had soon travelled to the Holy Land where I found work with the Israel Antiquities Authority, the British School of Archaeology in Jerusalem and with the Palestinian department of Antiquities in order to get a balanced view of the importance of art to each group.

I was profoundly affected by the physical beauty of the land history and rituals of Jews, Christians, Muslims and Bahais – but I felt that something was missing. There was a split between sacred and secular society and conflicts between people due to their literal interpretations of their own scripture but a loose interpretation of the scriptures of other religions.

At Easter in the Church of the Holy Sepulchre I was amazed as a symbolic effigy of Christ was ritually processioned, crucified, anointed and then laid in the tomb. At Christmas in the Church of the Nativity in Bethlehem I was deeply touched as I sat with nuns and monks around an effigy of the infant Christ at the reputed site of his birth.

My investigation was not limited to a consideration of the traditional western religion. From the ages of 14 to 17 I had experimented with Jewish Qabbalah and Chaos Magick (a system of ritual magic influenced by Aliastair Crowley). In my twenties I visited Hindu, Buddhist and Sikh places of worship.

A founder of Chaos Magick, Pete Carroll, states that

> "Chaos Magic concentrates upon technique. Underlying all systems from Witchcraft to Tibetan Sorcery, that the eclectically minded magician may use, there is a fundamental unity of practical technique depending on visualisation, the creation of thought entities and altered states of consciousness achieved by either quiescent or ecstatic meditations. The eclectic point of view implies that belief itself can be regarded as a technique for achieving one's aims. A further implication of the principle of relativity of belief is that all beliefs are considered to be arbitrary and contingent." (1)

These varied ritual experiments led to some interesting experiences but I felt that a conceptual framework needed establishing. The question that was foremost in my mind in my late teens and early twenties was why does anything exist at all, why isn't there just a nothingness?

I felt that this question was resolved when I had a mystical experience of non-duality – beyond conceptual oppositions such as being and nothingness. I came to believe that nothingness was just as much a concept as being and if one concept should exist then it seems make sense it should be "being" and that this being might be associated with goodness. My mystical experience was of a transcendence of moral struggle but moralism was the tradition that I believed in so I could not accept the mystics' path.

David K. Clark & Norman L. Gleisler, two Christian theologians, argue for this theistic position.

> "In the context of knowledge, the mystical consciousness of New Age pantheists entangles them in difficulties. Pantheists who use a mystical way of knowing must try somehow to distinguish tow modes of knowing, the mystical mode and the empirical mode. The first of these is unitive, unmediated, nonconceptual, nonlogical and noninferential. By contrast, the second is divided, conceptual, logical and inferential." (2)

> ""Pantheism feels a constant rational pressure to take an extreme view: evil is not real." Either evil is real (and in God) or evil is not real. The first option is unpleasant. Who wants to say God is or contains evil? The second option is left. Though pantheists resist this conclusion, the inner logic of pantheism inexorably presses them toward the illusionist view of evil." (3)

To understand how these issues relate to contemporary art it is useful to look at Derrida's distinction between Messianicity and the Chora. Derrida sees messianicity as not necessarily religious but as a rupture in horizons of expectation. Messianism is linked to a faith in universal justice. This faith is a rational realisation that belief in rational systems is not founded on the laws contained in the system of laws. It is a mystical origin that is spontaneous and quasi automatic. But this messianic faith in allowing of uprooting from dogmatism allows universal rationality and political democracy by looking expectantly to new faith perspectives. Derrida views religion as Abrahamic and related to Jewish, Christian and Muslim faiths. In contrast Derrida considers the Chora to be Greek He describes it as an empty space as used by Plato and Plotinus and continued by Heidegger. This Chora is seen as a desert and a Nothing, it is a realm of possibility that can be revealed in opposition to the actual revealing of religion. (4)

Art theorists have favoured the Chora but not Messianicity. "Chora" was an exhibition curate by Sue Hubbard and Simon Morley and featured 12 artists in London, Bath, Bracknell and Kendal in 2000. In the exhibition book "Chora" Cheryl Cooper in "Aporais of chora" notes that in "Revolution in Poetic Language" Julia Kristeva sees the Chora as a place of open possibility where masculine Form is joined with feminine Matter. Chora is seen as a feminine and maternal source that the created world comes from. (5)

There is an assumption that this Chora and maternity is superior to the masculine and this is where my work disagrees. My work seeks to channel possibility concerning spirituality into a definite religious form in Messianicity.

A theoretical framework for "liminal" art work that relates to the Chora can also be seen in "Liminal Acts A Critical Overview of Contemporary Performance and Theory" by Susan Broadhurst Cassel Published April 2000.

> "liminal performance similarly presents a deconstruction of binary opposition, which is demonstrated in the collapse of hierarchical distinctions such as those between high and mass/popular culture. Central to the liminal is a mixing of popular knowledge with "elitist" knowledge, together with a definite blurring of set boundaries; in other worlds a certain intertextuality is presented. Other aesthetic features that are present in the liminal and parallel Nietzsche's "active interpretation" are playfulness and the celebration of the surface "depthlessness of culture", together with a stylistic bricolage and the mixing of codes. (6)

This mixing resembles the idea that religion is a Wittgenstinian language game but with so many different games how are we to choose which to play? Broadhurst says that Lyotard sees these games as relating to shorter phrases but she thinks that these phrases are significatory and not the liminality that is a semiotic space of aesthetic possibility.

Lyotard's "theorization, as I argue, falls short in one important way: it is premised primarily on a linguistic model. This proves ultimately untenable in the face of such intersemiotic practices as the liminal." (7)

Broadhurst does not consider the liminality of mixing semiotic with the symbolic. Broadhurst believes liminal creations can have a cultural effect by creating new visions of possibility outside of what is expected in society but she does not spell out what this might mean.

Methods

I believe, however, that the liminal state is between normal consciousness and mystical consciousness and that it is an in-determinacy conducive to return a person to the mystical. However, if the mystical is not returned to then if something is not offered as a replacement for the mystical then evil meanings may be generated to fill the vacuum, so to counter this I began to look at alternative good meanings in an analysis of art and world history. I called my analysis The Ism.

To do this I created work that artistically expressed my innermost concerns about religion. A pattern began to emerge from my own work and I applied this pattern to world religions and their art forms. This pattern was that began to make abstract, colourful, and process based environments that I felt corresponded to the Dionysian mystical consciousness and figurative and sculptural products that I felt corresponded to the Apollonian moral consciousness.

By coincidence Broadhurst describes Nietzsche's characterisation of Apollonian and Dionysian.

"Apollo is associated with form and structure; the pure artistic expression of the Apollonian principle is sculpture. By contrast, Dionysis is associated with energy, sexuality, fertility and nature; the pure Dionysian art is music." (8)

Broadhurst sees liminal art as Dionysian (i.e. mystical) whereas I focus art relating to Messianicity that is Apollonian (ie Moral).

Beginning my MA in Theory of Contemporary Art and Performance with Wimbledon School of Art gave a new direction in my work. This was the inclusion of popular culture. In my performance work this began by the use of disco lights, mirror balls and neon signs. With an an interest in how the popular culture seemed to be a horizontal levelling of high art's concerns I saw how this might resemble the mystic's universal ordinariness, where everything is recognised as having the same essence, in this case where everything becomes a popular consumer product.

In response I developed "Club Religion" events in 2002, incorporating popular cultural forms of kitsch clubbing, music, fashion and sculpture. "Club Religion" was a space where religious and secular faiths can come together in open-minded possibility, but recognises that the energy needs to be channelled into a positive moral effect and not just a hedonistic aesthetic experience.

My recent exhibition "Stop Armageddon" was in the venue I had received my calling to go to the Holy Land. It was at the Quaker Gallery, near Trafalgar Square, and coincided with the Anti War demonstrations (March 2003) which I took part in. I designed the exhibition as a domestic space with nursery, playroom and television lounge. Manikins sat in the lounge as if watching my DVD of the birth of Eve II the Disco Art Messiah. Eve II is a doll I filmed myself dressing in Star of David nappies, then painting with a rainbow swastika and crowning with disco boppers at Ground Zero, New York. Here she was in a nursery with her interreligious mobile and golden disco crib. In the play room was the "New Jerusalem", an interreligious playset. (N.B. see cover of book)

By creating Eve II the negative and destructive energies at Ground Zero were given a new symbolic, narrative content. Eve II returned a Big Apple (New York) to the tree of knowledge of good and evil and found the tree of life (world economic aid). This new Eden is opposed to the tree of death that invading Eden (associated with Mesopotamia and Iraq) has generated. The crib was situated between two Christmas trees, one with fairy lights (the tree of life) and one with plastic apple and inflatable snake (tree of knowledge). Above the crib was a neon sign spelling "GOD?" and a large golden birthday balloon of the number 0, symbolising the mystical void, the Chora.

With Eve II I symbolically join the Judaeo Christian narrative tradition of a masculine Messiah with the feminine mystical tradition by way of the rainbow swastika painted on her chest. This is not the Nazi war symbol but a Hindu symbol of peace and good luck and is the symbol of Divali (the Hindu equivalent of Christmas). I painted Eve II with this symbol at Ground Zero to mark how the destruction of the Twin Towers could be a catalyst for the first world seeing its position in the global scheme.

Eve II was given the play role of founder of "New Jerusalem", a playset mixing together kitsch religious buildings and figures. A Dome of the Rock alarm clock sat on top of a record turntable next to a cardboard model of the Jewish Temple whilst visitors raced Jesus and Krishna on scalextric cars.

The idea was that even a child could join together the different faiths, so why do adults kill each other over religion? Religions are treated like games that are united by the common language of kitsch but the viewer is reminded that there is a gulf between the kitsch ideals and the reality as "GOD?" in neon oversees the scene and the rainbow swastika highlights the problematic nature of faith. It brings up the question of how a God could allow the Holocaust.

I was dressed up in the exhibition as an interreligious prophet of Disco Art Religion. I sat outside the gallery and marched on the anti-war demonstration, standing at the base of Nelson's Column with a banner stating "the nigh of the end is world" breaking down the phrase and reflecting the break down in faith in our political system.

My work contains immense generalisations but this is the point of the work, that in an artistic joining together of the material culture of religions we can overlook the strict specifics and divisions of religions and scriptures. But for the work to become a threat to dogmatic structures it needs to generate sufficient interest with open minded people.

Exhibition Context

The notion of celebrity and leadership are important as Eve II, a doll, is an attempt to break down the idea of religious leaders and gods. Recent examples of contemporary art trends can be seen in the paintings of Sharon Lutchman, where she depicts Victoria and David Beckham as the gods Shiva and Parvati and also David Beckham as a 14th century Icon of Jesus. In contrast to this I would depict Jesus or Buddhas as David Beckham, to express how religious figures are like secular heroes. Racing Jesus against Krishna and presenting religious manikins as fashion figures and pop stars makes a reverse move of showing how religious high culture can be broken down into less revered cultural forms. This move links the masculine patriarch of religion to the feminine, to the everyday but still over it as the emphasis is still on religion.

In contrast we can look at the political relation of celebrity Brit Art with atheism and punk rock at the new Saatchi Gallery, at County Hall, London. Just like punk rock, Brit Art had an association with the glamorisation of crime and violence, and both have become a part of the British establishment. Punk and Brit Art arose in a Thatcherist capitalist atmosphere associated with individual freedom over social concern. Saatchi contributed to this atmosphere in his advertising campaigns for the conservative party.

Gavin Turk's "Pop" is a life-sized waxwork sculpture of the artists dressed as Sid Vicious. He watches over the entrance to the central exhibition. The suffering and fatality of life is shown in the varied works, but could Saatchi actually do something tin influence artistic agendas to change that suffering?

The most telling statement of Saatchi's exhibition comes from Richard Wilson's "20:50" oil tank installation, which sits waist high in one of the wood panelled rooms. Visitors must enter one at a time to see the work and leave all bags at the door. It is like entering a religious shrine, to commune with the black gold. The gallery building used to be the offices for the London Council and the oil perfectly reflects the walls and is a symbol of the establishment reflecting on itself. Charles Saatchi is from a Jewish family that came from Baghdad, Iraq when he was four years old. Saatchi has been expanding his cultural property, similar to US globalization and oil expansionism in the Middle East. Saatchi's art collecting could be seen as a statement of complicity in capitalist expansion.

Sculptural Context

An artwork purchased by Saatchi for £1 million is Jake and Dinos Chapman's model of "Hell", which shows fantasized horrors of the Holocaust made as toy models. In contrast Eve II is a doll that symbolically asks if the Jewish messiah would be able to forgive those atrocities. The rough construction of my "New Jerusalem" scalextric is in contrast to the neurotic precision of the Chapman's "Hell", showing it to be more a piece of conceptual art linked to postmodern breakdown rather than a statement of modernist regimentation. Eve II refers to a childlike state where the religions seen to be truly religious because they are coming together.

My new Eden has a religious playset in which kitsch model buildings and figures of gods are cut in half and mixed up as postmodern hybrids. This contrast with the Zygotes in the Chapman's Eden called "Six Feet Under". These Zygotes are manikins of children that are cut up and reassembled, joined like Siamese twins, with multiple limbs wearing trainers and with protruding penises and anuses for noses and mouths. They are mutations of consumerism and show a naked sexuality twisting into unnatural forms. They represent a selfish, mutated capitalist domination of nature. They breaking down social structures but offer nothing to replace them. In contrast, my new Eden is one of a union of all humanity in a world of trade equality.

At the entrance to my exhibition I displayed a family of manikins wearing mixed up items of religious clothing in a series of mock fashion adverts. This family of manikins contrasts that of the Chapman's family only my figures are placed under robes of religion to protect their modesty and keep at least some religious ideals.

The Chapmans look at how society has mutated our bodies and in "Performance: Live Art Since the 60's" RoseLee Goldberg Thames and Hudson 1998, Goldberg states:

"it would take almost thirty years of feminist scholarship to unravel the very different uses of the body by male and female artist of this period, and properly to credit the women artist for their pioneering and highly considered examination of the body as a measure of identity, taboo, and the limits of masculine/feminine emancipation, their belief in the body as prime, raw material, opened numerous territories for artistic investigation." (90)

This work included Hermann Nitsch's Dionysian animal sacrifices and Ron Athey's sado-masochistic photographs reconstructing sexualised versions of the lives of Martyrs and Saints.

In both my work and that of the Chapmans the live art and blood of the body is replaced with the dead art using manikins. These are symbols of the end of a search for meaning and reality and the acceptance that consumerism is now dominant. The religion is dead but instead of being like the Chapmans and just accepting this, I try to return religion to life, and explore the idea of messianicity.

Performance Context

At my "Stop Armageddon" exhibition I used Eve II in a ritual to sacrifice a small plastic model of a red heffer in a model of the Jewish Temple (the sacrifice of a real red heffer is needed to restore the Temple sacrifice in Jerusalem). Once split in two I installed this model in the Temple as a miniature Damien Hirst sculpture. I turned the ritual sacrifice into child's play in order to deflate high seriousness of performance art so that artist did not get stuck in a Dionysian emphasis on sexuality, fertility and nature.

My other rituals involve the audience in icing a cake whilst dressed in rainbow coloured robes and under disco lighting. This links together the Holy Communion and a children's birthday party to show how universal the energies involved in ritual are, but when they become too structure with belief systems they lose their immediacy. Whilst rituals need belief systems I also trivialise these so that the authentic structure behind them can appear. The liturgy of Catholic rituals needs explaining by my rituals are accessible even to children as they take the form of a child's birthday celebration. This develops the general structure of religious ritual into a specific form that remains domestic and accessible.

Some might criticise this by saying that they have outgrown both children's parties and religious rituals. In response to this I think that the purpose of the work is to try and rekindle the child-like hope and optimism that things are worth celebrating and can be changed for positive effect by faith and that there is a mystery to the world that cannot be solved and closed off by adults.

My interactive rituals stem from the audience involvement in 1960's happenings with their mystical philosophy of non-dualistic inclusion. The Blue Man Group was formed in 1987 with a series of happenings and they also have fun, audience participatory performances. "Tubes" has been showing in New York since 1992 and has 3 men painted blue, performing tricks and ironic satire on contemporary society and art. Damien Hirst style spin paintings are made by spitting paint onto canvases and paint flies into the air as the performers bang large drums with paint on the skins of the drums. They take members of the audience onto stage to take part in surreal comedy experiments such as wearing vests linked with tubes, so that when the participant eats a pieced of cake given to them liquefied cake comes spouting out of their chest. The climax of the show has the audience pulling large rolls of crepe paper from above their heads and having these streamers cover the whole theatre.

The ironic satire is further shown by having 3 red digital display tubes with different messages on them, inviting you to choose which one to read. The boards cross-reference each other and the audience become confused as they try to read all 3. These display boards are then used to drum with and the effect is spectacular as they turn signs that provide meaning into purely aesthetic objects. There are also projections of fractal geometry and the emphasis is on the break down of human absolutes into pure abstractions. The celebratory experience is universalised by having abstract, blue performers, but they provide the audience with no specific identity to take back into the world. The show is an abstract entertainment with no lasting meaning.

Mixed Media Content

An artist who combines visual and performance art is Revd. Ethan Acres. He combines an evangelic type preaching with varied art forms to convey his message. He is a licensed preacher from the United States who has worked from a mobile church.

His underlying philosophy is a reconciliation of opposites. He put the light side and the shadow side together in a performance in the Turbine Hall at Tate Modern. There he dresses as a preacher, dragging a fellow performer behind him. The fellow performer was dressed as a shadow and was attached to Revd Acres by the ankles. As a symbol of union Revd Acres rolled down the Turbine Hall with the Shadow. Acres then shed his priestly robes and skipped away free, dressed in an undersized Peter pan costume. He did not involve audience participation and this did not follow the breaking down of dualisms that he preached.

Revd Acres' links to music were shown in a performance made at the Eve Club in London's West End. This is the UK's only dance floor, with 1970's style disco light floor tiles and a bikini clad girl danced seductively around him. He placed his robes over the girl and came out of his robes dresses as a serpent. Again the emphasis was to accept the opposites.

Revd Acres uses kitsch and irony as the formats of his preaching and services but they also convey a serious message. They differ from my work in that I am trying to promote a moral perspective and not a mystical one that unites opposites. I also try to encompass more than just one belief system which simultaneously deconstructs exclusive truth claims about these religions but allows a space for a shared moral belief ground to appear – and not just a shared desire for mystical union.

Revd Acres is interesting as his tattoos and rock and roll influences make him appear as if at home in a techno-shaman club but his performance acts show him like a "queen" in a gay disco. This union and his non-dualistic message show that his work relates to a mystical breakdown of traditional religious moral identities.

Club Context

Techno Shamanism clubs tend to have Pagan or Eastern religious themes. In the UK club nights include "Escape from Samsara", "Kundalini", "Tribalism" and "Planet Angel". These clubs contain group activities such as painting on walls, interactive video games, visual projections and immersive lighting (that creates psychedelic environments). Girls bring around cakes to eat and club goes can play with Lego. Performances include drumming, juggling and ribbon twirling. The emphasis in these clubs is on hallucinogens, Ecstasy and dancing. To create an atmosphere to induce states of trance the clubs have very loud, techno, tribal rhythms as well as areas for people to "chill out" and relax.

In contrast examples of Gay clubs with a religious theme are "Heaven", "Salvation", "Sanctuary" and (on the Asian gay scene) "Club Kali". These clubs often pay limited reference to the religious traditions that they are named after and focus on the kitsch visuals of the tradition, rejecting any deeper meaning. There is an interest in alcohol, dancing and sexual encounter in these clubs. The male clubs also have a hind of sado-masochistic leather boy image. This image has a relation also to S&M and Nazi memorabilia. The gay scene is often symbolized with a rainbow flag. The rainbow is a symbol that this clubbing scene has in common with the New Age clubbing scene.

The club scene in opposition to the religious rituals of the church because their own "rituals" of clubbing are concerned with self-expression, pleasure and free experience. It is ritualized but it is not ritual for the promotion of ideas held in faith, rather it is for the promotion of sensual experience.

Many churches have been converted into use for clubs and bars, in particular the crypt in St. Matthews Church, Brixton. Other churches have become art spaces that also function like clubs, such as the 291 Gallery on Hackney road, where exhibitions and performances occur.

Art venues like the ICA are host to a number of music club nights, where the emphasis is often put on making links between music from around the world. Nights such as the Jewish/Arab "Naming the Golem" make these links but they are always kept firmly in a secular context. Religious music and artistic expression are rejected.

My work is celebratory and uses this energy for the reconciliation of cultural and religious opponents. I have held discos as part of my rituals, electronically mixing disco with religious music. My "Disco Art Religion" is not a religion as it is about he bringing together of both religious and secular culture they follow a moral model where people can instantly recognize the importance of breaking down divisions between people. This is a moral argument. I explained the meaning of work to the viewers in order to shift he emphasis back to historical narrative and to give the work its religious context and the responses to my work were brilliant.

I had begun my journey from the Quaker meeting house, to explore the relation of art and religion in Jerusalem and had returned there to mount an exhibition of my vision of a "New Jerusalem" where the religious forms are valued and important but should not interfere with human relations and co-operation. Within seconds of closing the door on my exhibition the bulb of the main disco light behind my neon "GOD?" blew out. Was this a sign from God?

Criticisms

1. The work may be considered blasphemous by the groups it is seeking to include.

I feel, however, that a multicultural, religious society should allow articulation of blasphemy just as a secular societies allows accusation against them from religious groups. Compromise is necessary if people are to be brought together and I reduce other cultures because I feel that the western intellectual model fits best the project that I am doing and also has a masculine conceptual structure. This imperialistic structure, is however, tempered by the use of art and feminine aesthetics. It is honest about this inequality rather than pretending it is not there.

One Muslim criticised my Dome of the Rock on a record turntable for being blasphemous but I said that it was just an idol and that I was breaking down idolatry. As well as making this breakdown I am also celebration of faith in its variety of expressions. It is not a sexual or disrespectful break down but was also trying to maintain a remnant of genuine faith.

2. The links that I want to make cannot be made easily by art but require years of building relations and so my work has no spiritual depth.

I feel, however, that by taking in too many specific details then religious division is created. Art is being used to break down theologically un-surmountable barriers and deep spirituality is present in the act of bringing people together. There will always be a division between people that want to come together and people that do not want any co-operation. All that can be done with people who want to continue division is to demonstrate the advantages of co-operation.

Kitsch concerns a certain superficiality and lack of depth. It represents a mass-production and a common sentiment, often of a naive quality. The ability to appreciate it is often associated with a lack of taste. I have chosen kitsch because it relates to a created material rather than a deeper inner spirituality. It allows the following of outward ritualized forms than inner experience. The religions that are represented with kitsch objects are often dogmatic and so, by combining them, a religious possibility for tolerance and co-operation is expressed.

3. There is a large gap between what I intend in the work and its real effect.

Whilst I do not know if my rituals are effective the people participating enjoy themselves and come together in unity. They appeal to a sense of fun as well as being visually very stimulating. At first it seems that the religious effects are secondary as people are caught up in the aesthetic enjoyment. However, participants are presented with a genuine religious ritual option, whether they accept that or not. Its efficacy is up to the individual and this makes the work is open to both believer and non-believer. My neon "GOD?" has a question mark, not because it is agnostic but because there is a decision to suspend judgement for the purpose of coming together in moral community, thus placing morals about individual religious views of who God is.

Prior to existential choice there is an openness and uncertainty. The work allows people to celebrate in this uncertainty whilst guiding them to a religious choice and helping them to value the choice that they eventually make.

4. It seems that many people are cynical about the statements of contemporary art.

It seems as though people cannot see a political or aspirational use to contemporary art. They see it as being more than just aesthetic but do not associate with the message that it provides. Viewing dirt, sex and death is a therapeutic exercise for the rich classes because it balances their lives but also allows them superiority over the middle classes whose more refined (but still representational and kitsch) art serves them in their goal to become like the rich classes. My work is a clear message and provides a clear aesthetic. It does not make a claim beyond itself and provides a model for the world. It is a conceptual statement but does not claim to be the product of immense skill. It contains work that is the product of skill as a validation of whether work is important. The statements it makes are about the formation of a new paradigm. Skilled work around this paradigm can be produced when there is acceptance or interest in the concept of the paradigm by an art world that can fund the production of such work. This is part of the responsibility of the buying art world, just as it is the responsibility of the first world to create an economic change.

Creating alternative consumer options won't change the main power structure but it may change perceptions of rulers or young people who are potential rulers. Aesthetic considerations can guide political decisions and increased understanding, appreciation and integration of world religions might increase opportunities available to marginalized groups which may lead to increased opportunities for countries around the world.

In conclusion I feel that a relation between opposites provides an interesting way to look at contemporary art and performance. I think that some contemporary art practice has too strong a focus on the synthesis of opposites and does not provide a model for difference. I think that this is perhaps because the first world s economically divided from the rest of the world's cultures and psychologically balances by adopting an integrational model in an apolitical art. Messianicity and religion are based on the hope and faith that the world can politically change for the better. They set an ideal to be worked towards as opposed to a contemporary art view that seeks to make the everyday or the sexual into idealized art.

21st April 2003 (with slight amendments)

Essay 6.

THE RELATION BETWEEN THEORY AND PRACTICE OF THE WORK OF THOMAS HIRSCHHORN WITH SPECIFIC REFERENCE TO ART AND POPULAR CULTURE.

Interviewed for the catalogue of the 50th Venice Biennale (2003) Immanueal Wallerstein (author of "Utopistics") **(1)** stated that the term Utopia was invented by Sir Thomas More in the 16th century and means "nowhere" in Greek. He said that a Utopia is seen as being an impossible place and an act of imagination concerning what a good society should look like.

I would like to suggest that Hirschhorn's work shows a rejection of utopian thinking but celebrates the energy it has against consumer society. I think that this Utopian speculation can also be seen as a new trend in international contemporary art but I want to suggest that non-materialist perspectives need to be considered as a way out of the impasse.

Okuwi Enwezor suggested, in "The Black Box", his introduction to the exhibition catalogue for "Documenta XI" (2002), that Ground Zero is a site that appears to define politics and art for the 21st century. He suggests that it is both a destruction of an old perspective and a tabula rasa where a new perspective can be built **(2)**.

Thomas Hirschhorn's *Cavemanman* 2002 was his first major show in New York and I suggest that the womb-like *Cavemanman* could represent the birth (or defecation) of the viewer back out of a cultural tabula rasa / Ground Zero into the world of consumerism – with nothing left but an energy for change.

Cavemanman (at the Barbara Gladstone Gallery, New York 2002) was a cave made of wrapping tape and cardboard. As I entered the Chelsea white cube gallery I was placed in an environment where nothing was left uncovered. It was like entering a theatrical set. I moved around the space, I walked up ramps, along levels and into subsidiary grottoes and cul-de-sacs. In my explorations I had to negotiate around boulders and rocks made out of cardboard boxes covered in masking tape. The fantasy construction was interrupted by finding academic texts included within the walls, some with fake sticks of dynamite attached – suggesting that political change occurs only by violent means.

The central grotto of the cave system was a "living" space where a "tribe" of shop dummy type figures was covered with gold tin-foil. They were linked by umbilical like, foil tentacles to books such as John Rawls *Theory of Justice* and to fake bombs. Rawls is seen as reintroducing the study of the political philosophy at a time (1960s) when philosophers rejected such study in favour of logical positivism and a study of scientific facts - so this could represent a world of idealistic thinking, supported by violence.

On the walls of the cave was repeatedly written, in graffiti, the basic theory that "1 man = 1 man". This gives the title of the work "Cavemanman" but also links to hippy idealism of the 60's by ending with the word "man". "1man=1man" suggested equality but also market value and inter-changeability. The utopian idealism in the phrase was represented as doomed to failure as cans of coke and sprite littered the floor in an excess of cultural waste.

The tin-foil family in the cave might represent us all as being consumers in a failed idealism. Hirschhorn seems to suggest that human nature has an urge to consume and is a commodity itself. I think that Hirschhorn is perceptive of our current dilemma as with no idealistic or utopian possibilities present to us we are left with assuming that we are part of a commodity system. When we leave the gallery we are symbolically re-born, from the womb-like cave, back into the world as brand new consumers.

In an essay in the *Village Voice*, entitled *More Is More*, **(3)** Kim Levin likens the cave to an intestinal tract and I think that this reinforces Hirschhorn's interest in using trash and "low" materials– as intensines process food into waste. Levins feels that the dramatic juxtaposition of idealism and physical trash reinforces Hirschhorn's presentation of the failure of Utopianism – represented as ancient history unfulfilled in empty consumerism.

Other artists who use packaging materials and rubbish to look at social ideals are Michael Landy and Tomoto Takahashi.

In *High Art Lite* Julian Stallabrass says that Landy invented his own fictional corporate identity, it is "Scrapheap Services" and aims to clear away surplus people from society. In "Scrapheap Services" (1995) "dummies dressed in corporate cleaning uniforms sweep up thousands of tiny human figures cut out from drink cans, McDonald's packaging and other detrituis" **(4)**. The tiny figures are stamped with corporate colours and logos. The viewers are implicated in the situation and have to stand on the cut out figures as they walk around. Here Landy makes a direct social comment - asking if our consumer society properly cares for people.

In an uncredited article in Tate Magazine, Issue 3 is a description of Landy's "Breakdown" 2001. An empty department store in Oxford Street, London, was converted into a factory for the systematic destruction of all of Landy's possessions. Each possession was itemised and then shredded by a team of operators working a conveyor belt and shredder. This act of rejection seems to be an attempt to escape from the effects of commodification but Landy's new work transforms his line of thought. This work is a series of etchings of common weeds and is called "Nourishment". The weeds have been collected from urban sites over the past two years and are a laborious study that refers more to botanical works than to romantic high art. **(5)** This seems to suggest a guarded optimism that is a natural growth arising out of a complete rejection of consumerism. Even out of the crack of consumerism it seems that "real" life can arise. In contrast, Hirschhorn's work suggests that we cannot escape consumerism.

Stallabrass also describes how Tomoko Takahashi creates complex three dimensional installations and collages out of waste materials. "Beaconsfield" 1997 was an installation where trash was laid on the floor of a darkened gallery space and separated into sections by white lines. The trash was lit by an assortment of lamps and standing lights. Machines in the installation eg. slide projector and tape recorder, continually played and on an old telephone face was written the word "process" **(6)**. The work suggested that everything is subject to consumer ordering, including art.

In redisplaying "Beaconsfield" for the Saatchi show "New Neurotic Realism" in 1999 Takahashi made clear her ideas about the "process" of constructing the work, - seemingly halted at an arbitrary point, to show the continual process of creation **(7)**. Stallabras thinks that by showing the construction, cost, labour and issues of ownership criticism of the commodification of art were made.

I think that, like Takahashi, Hirschhorn shows the waste of commodification but also, like Landy, he wants to very explicitly reject this system, and sees the use of rubbish as a possible way to do this, by connecting to the *informe* - the formless.

In "Formless – A Users Guide" Yve-Alain Bois and Rosalind Krauss say that "The other word to which Bataille turned to evoke this process of "deviance" was *informe*, a de-classing in every sense of the term:" **(8)** This de-classing was a breaking down of hierarchies of form and matter to produce an entropy, a homogenized, horizontal levelling that is a way "of liberating our thinking from the semantic, the servitude to thematics," **(9)** In other words it is a rejection of high ideals and oppressive systems by using low and accessible materials.

Hirschhorn uses this theory and, to coincide with his *Bataille Monument* at Documenta XI, he commissioned Christopher Fiat to write an essay on Bataille, called "The Experience of Violence in Sacrifice" **(10)**. This described Batailles' rejection of ideas of commodification and related to the semi-sacrificial/altar spaces that Hirschhorn creates to suggest an energy that cannot be commodified.

Hirschhorn uses ideas of the formless to politically reject commodity. He states that

> "To make art politically means to choose materials that do not intimidate, a format that doesn't dominate, a device that does not seduce. To make art politically is not to submit to an ideology or to denounce the system, in opposition to so-called

"political art". It is to work with the fullest energy against the principle of quality." **(11)**

The energy of Hirschhorn's work is intended to overload and to confuse the viewer – breaking down their political assumptions and expressing their inability to process and to control the world.

Hirschhorn joins both elite/academic theory and popular kitsch by transforming them both into trash. Hirschhorn puts general theoretical objects (eg. books and pages) and popular objects (eg. baseball caps and Rolex watches) inside low materials (eg. masking tape and cardboard). The theories and objects are transformed into garbage to show their consumer nature as commodities. By using trash I think that Hirschhorn critiques consumerism and challenges the elitism of the art object.

In contrast to this formlessness is a consumer utopia that tries to deny the base qualities of humanity. In "McTopia: Eating Time" John O'Neill **(12)** describes McTopia as being an example of this. In this parody of McDonalds he thinks that the excretory/formless body is hidden by a uniform blandness of fast-food, décor, music and staff. Information, choices and freedom are minimized by giving consumers small, standardised menu options. The meal produces indigestion but dissent is removed and only resurfaces in reaction to the low wages and harsh economic realities outside.

This kind of picture of consumerism, as social control through using shallow imagery, was theorized by Guy Debord and called the Spectacle. In his book on "Guy Debord" Anselm Tappe says that the Spectacle is conceived as an ensemble of independent, commodity representations. The spectator is separate from these images and is an isolated individual. **(13)** The spectacular society tries to deny a view of history as being part of a dialectical progression **(14)** but Debord thinks that direct communication between people can break down the Spectacle. **(15)** Thus opposition to the Spectacle appears to be dialectical (critical) thinking and improved personal relations (without commodity as an alienating intermediary).

An artistic attempt to critique the society of the Spectacle can be seen in urban pastoral art. Stallabras suggests that the pastoral is the view that simple living often produces values and truths which more sophisticated people have lost site of. **(16)** Richard Billingham's book "Rays A Laugh" 1996 provides a good example of the pastoral put into an urban context, with his photographic documentation of his family who live on a council estate. Stallabras suggests that his work is pastoral because the depictions of his family show that their lives express to us some truth that they are not fully aware of. **(17)**

Stallabras, however, criticises this kind of work as being fashionable but with no real political comment. **(18)** Roberts in "Domestic Squabble" is more sympathetic. He suggests that the localism and micro-narratives of this kind of work are in opposition to Globalism and the promise of grand narratives with their "Hegelian big sweeps of periods and epochs." **(19)** He concludes that they showed the gap that existed between the lives of ordinary people and the promises of critical theory, but in doing this have also rejected the vocabulary for making critical statements **(20)**.

In "Society of the Spectacle", Rebel Press 1987 **(21)** Guy Debord states that when the Spectacular society begins to critique itself that this then puts the notions of the Spectacle at a level of non-thought – ie. they become assumed and are an "official amnesia". This amnesia can be non-dialectical critique or pure advertising as both involve submissive thought. I think that Stallabras might suggest that urban pastoral art can be seen as contributing to this amnesia as it is not critical.

I think that the ability to overcome this kind of amnesia that was explored by Walter Benjamin in his views, which preceded the idea of the Spectacle.

In "Dream World of Mass Culture" Susan Buck-Morss says that Benjamin proposed that the world of images produced by consumer society has a limited life and is continually replaced by newer fashions and images. This change opens up the idea of radical, rather than just superficial, change that lies at an unconscious, mythic, level in human beings. This mythic change was not to return to a (pre-industrial) nature but was a radical reconstruction of the fragmented reality of industrial society. **(22)** This reconstruction was linked on an artistic level to surrealist montage - although Benjamin did not agree with artistic individualism as he thought that the collective is the source of a revolutionary energy. **(23)**

> "The trick in Benjamin's fairy tale is to interpret out of the discarded dream images of mass culture a politically empowering knowledge of the collective's own unconscious past" **(24)**

This knowledge is noted in "Dream City and Dream House, Dreams of the Future, Anthropological Nihilism, Jung" where Walter Benjamin **(25)** states that the waking being is aware of its concrete historical situation by placing itself in a politically empowered, critical, dialectical ideology of progress.

In "The press release & alternative spaces" Mark Harris says **(26)** how in "Ocean Floor" 1996 (produced for their exhibition *Dog-U-Mental*) the artist collective BANK presented a pastiche of this critical theory. They satirise attempts to create mythic alternatives and to dialectically combine opposites ,to create liminal spaces of open possibilities. These dreamlike constructions are criticised for giving no political direction and for just being promotions of commercial artists.

BANK also sent a press-release about *Mask of Gold* 1997 as a way to criticise the idea of the urban pastoral and of liminality. It criticised "non-art-looking-art" that was a study of oppression in other peoples lives but remained part of the middle-management structure that they were pretending to criticise.

Stallabras **(27)** notes that BANK parodies the corporate structure of commercial art and although it operates in the same way as FCUK's advertising campaigns – using anti-commercial statements to advertise themselves - Stallabras believes that BANK is consistent in its condemnation of art institutions. I think, however, that because BANK's work resembles the work they criticise (and because they do not suggest any alternatives) then BANK is open to all the criticism it makes of contemporary art.

Theodor Adorno and Max Horkheimer in "The Culture Industry" described the dreams of mass culture as being empty stylisation that involves cheap parody and not the transcendent asceticism of high culture. **(28)** Adorno thought that low culture creates individuals who seek identity by imitating manufactured capitalist stars and uses humour to promote resignation to oppressed conditions. **(29)** Thus, only dialectical, critical, thinking can give alternatives to popular culture. It seems to me that Stallabaras' position seems to reflect Adorno's views (which pre-dates Benjamin's), that critical (dialectical) leadership/culture should be given to people and that it should not be influenced by popular culture.

It seems to me that Hirschhorn turns Adorno type "elite theorists" into Benjamin style "mythic figures" that arise out of a critique of the trash of the spectacular society. It is as if Hirschhorn turns Adorno's position on its head by transforming great thinkers (and their theories) into idols similar to pop music idols.

It is the theorists' revolutionary, popular energy (and not their ideas) that he celebrates. But for Hirschhorn dialectical theory has reached an impasse and only the uncritical energy of the theorist offers hope. The hope is that there is a possibility of a new social system that can be achieved through creative political action.

The theorist is given the paraphernalia of being a popular figure with shrines, and objects of devotion. The difference between theory and art practice is broken down, as is the difference between art and popular objects. Hirschhorn 's work survives as art (and theory), in tension, by deconstructing its own authority as art (and theory).

Hirschhorn's altar displays (e.g., *Mondrian Altar*, 1997; *Ingeborg Bachmann Altar*, 1998; *Otto Freundlich Altar*, 1998) are homages to the tragically failed figures and projects of modernity that opposed commercial individualism with models of collective action. Buchloch says that such altars demonstrate that artists are bound up with forms of mass-engineered adulation and although it can exposes mass celebrity it also remains within it. **(30)**

Hirschhorn described his "fan" monument to Georges Bataille (*Bataille Monument*, Documenta XI, Kassel 2002) at the "Reports from the Fields of Visual Culture" conference at the Victoria Miro Gallery, London 2003. By putting the monument in a housing complex and not a historic site Hirschhorn critiqued the notion of a monument (and its location) as something that is fixed and grandiose. Batialle had nothing to do with Kassell and his monument could be shown anywhere. The monument had many different facets including a social complex of buildings, with library and exhibition. The Bataille sculpture was critiqued as being just a part of the monument and not the monument itself.

The library in the monument had books on subjects like art, sport and sex, but nothing on Bataille. This was in order to emphasise Bataille as a celebrity rather than his political writings and the exhibition gave information about the life of Bataille rather than his works. There was a snack bar that served as a focal point for the local community and a TV studio for local residents to make programmes about their day at the monument.

Hirschhorn saw himself as an equal co-worker. Residents were asked to help and were given pay and when the monument was dismantled the parts were taken by the residents. Hirschhorn physically put both theories and the public into his work, celebrating their formless energy - but I don't think that any critical direction remained from the project.

One attempt to theorise and give direction to the urban pastoral and the use of rubbish and the formless in art was made by Dave Beech and John Roberts in "Tolerating Impurities: An Ontology, Genealogy and Defence of Philistinism". They thought that the cultural term "Philistine" is usually seen as derogatory, and relating to deviance and an absence (31). They propose that it is a term that stands in opposition to terms of the "cultural" better, and changes as notions of culture change. This suggests that the high cultural rejection of mass media, sensual enjoyment and low materials, (for being "philistine") is open to reappraisal (32). Thus art can reclaims cultural elements that were formerly seen as being philistine and social change can occur through this process.

Stallabras thinks that that Beech and Roberts' "Philistine debate" supports urban pastoral artwork but that such artwork does not force a clear cultural definition or closure. Whilst it is often justified artistically for creating a liminality between cultural options Stallabras thinks that this serves no critical purpose. **(33)**

In contrast to this Malcolm Quinn in "The Legions of the Blind: the Philistine and Cultural Studies" suggests a critical use of the notion of the Philistine. He thinks that, by rejecting Adorno's elitism, art had lost its critical bite but that " Philistine" as a necessary term of cultural separation **(34)** reintroduces criticality to the notion of culture. Culture is seen the primary source of alienation in humanity because it contains within it **(35)** the idea of the philistine and so implies the idea of alienation that forms part of critical, Marxist thinking.

I think that this does not take critical thinking towards any specific theory and still leaves us with a liminality that is a point of impasse that critical (dialectical) thinking has reached through its merging of opposites. Stallabras criticises this liminality but I think that he fails to consider the possibility that art might be able to find a way beyond it. I think that solutions might be created out of this liminal space of open possibility and that these creations might resemble consumer choices.

It seems as if Hirschhorn wants to move beyond this dialectical impasse and chooses energy as the only available option. Some contemporary Utopian thinkers, however, propose using critical, Marxist thinking to regulate this energy.

In "The End of Socialism? The End of Utopia? The End of History?" Krishan Kumar thinks that although socialism failed in Europe its utopian ideals still remain part of the culture, ready to re-emerge as a counter to liberal, consumerist capitalism – which he thinks is too culturally and ecologically destructive. **(36)**

He thinks that postmodern spaces of consumer diversity are akin to Thomas More's 18th century, spatial vision of utopia rather than a historical, temporal progression as in Marx. He thinks that the postmodern consumer's movement between these varied, spatial, consumer cultures links to a temporal, regulatory Utopianism (I think that this is perhaps in a way similar to Benjamin's changing styles allowing the possibilities of the myth of revolution to appear).

He proposes a critical regulation of the national and international use of the earth's resources, with authoritarianism and communitarianism both featuring alongside liberal capitalism. **(37)**

In "Spaces of Hope" David Harvey also makes this difference between a temporal (critical, dialectical Marxist) versus a spatial (free-market, neo-liberal, capitalist) utopian space. He sees these as potentially united but doesn't want a closed capitalist system. Rather he wants the innovative change associated with capitalist experimentation to apply to the system as a whole. He thinks that ecological and social concerns are always subject to change and that a monopololistic capitalist system's attempt to create inflexible closure against this change might cause disaster. **(38)** I would like to suggest that relativistic choice in cultural studies relates to models of consumerism and that dialectical critical thinking in critical studies relates to models of Marxism. I think that this helps to clarify the different options.

In the exhibition catalogue of the 50th Venice Biennale, Immanueal Wallerstein combines Marxist, regulatory criticality with cultural relativism but I think that this openness is slightly confused as he uses dialectics to try and argue for the benefits of a cultural relativism that denies the universalising dialectical process of Marxism. Wallerstein said that he believes Marxism's appeal was that it rejected specific Utopian visions yet maintained Utopian aspirations - through its non-specific process of communal change. However I think that the systems inflexibility may be more problematic than a specific utopian goal as it cannot be shown as having failed in the same way. **(39)**

Kumar, Harvey and Wallerstein all suggest a consumerist cultural relativism regulated by a critical, Marxist, basis. Robert in "Philosophies of the Everyday" proposed that cultural relativism gives a cultural montage that has little political effect. Although the montages can give rise to counter cultures these counter cultures are absorbed as consumerist counter cultures separate from critical and emancipatory histories. **(40)** Thus dialectical regulations are required by Robert but for Hirschhorn no dialectical theories remain – just their energy.

I would like to point to Yoko Ono's work in the 50th Venice Biennale as it marks celebrity energy from the 70s and the 00's and also relates to Bonami's acknowledgement of the limited political effect of art in the Director's preface to the exhibition catalogue **(41)**. Ono's "Declaration of Nutopia" 1973 is a signed document made with John Lennon as ambassadors of a conceptual county that is everywhere. The document is stamped with a seal that pictures the seal of utopia playing with a ball.

This fun statement, with serious intent, was updated in Ono's "Imaginary Map Piece" 2002, a metal globe, painted in a haphazard way and graffiti style. **(42)** I presume that this is a statement about the breakdown of boundaries and borders. It fits with the artistic fashion for the formless but instead of a ball that is played with by a seal it is now a globe that is played with by the art world. The marks resemble the flight paths and connections of the international art world.

Just as the "Declaration of Nutopia" seems to have been an empty gesture so too does this globe. The idea that art is ineffectual might be acknowledged as the title "Imaginary Map Piece" uses "piece" rather than "peace".

Hirschhorn's work differs as he makes political figures into celebrities and not celebrities into political figures. Hirschhorn's *Flugplatz Welt/World Airport* at the 48th Venice Biennale, 1999, and the Renaissance Society at the University of Chicago, 2000, however, resembles Ono's globe as both works show energy with no specific direction.

The central installation is dominated with an airport landing strip, on tables. On the airstrip are large cardboard airplanes bearing corporate logos. In *Disguise the Limit: Thomas Hirschhorn's World Airport* Hamza Walker describes this as being "in direct contrast to the conflict displayed on the ten, evenly spaced partitions that march along the tarmac's edge." **(43)** The partitions show disasters and conflicts in third world countries.

Walker says that 4 altars are placed on the four corners of the installation. These altars link theory and popular commodities and "are dedicated to philosophy (mind), sports (body), and religion (soul)". These ideas are represented, by philosophical texts (by Georges Bataille, Gilles Deleuze and Felix Guattari, Antonio Gramsci, and Spinoza,); oversized athletic shoes (Adidas, Nike, Puma, Reebok); and articles devoted to various faiths (Christianity, Buddhism, Taoism). **(44)** Mind, body, and soul are contrasted to consumerism but are dominated by the runway's symbolism of material and corporate internationalism.

Within the installation are some giant tin-foil spoons that are associated with feeding and donation. A pool of painted blood seeps out from beneath the runway and the installation shows how history and social issue shave been built over with a jet-setting vision of homogenised, consumer modernism. Hirschhorn shows a diversity marginalized by a wasteful capitalist hegemony and critiques airport spaces for being ways to promote consumerism and globalisation.

In his introduction to "Documenta XI" Okuwi Enwezor called for a more inclusive and global art that addressed the marginalized ethnic groups and was process based, rather than making conclusive statements **(45)**. He viewed Ground Zero as a Tabula Rasa that characterised de-colonisation and introduced cultures on the periphery into the centre. He also called for a dialogue between Westernism and Islam. **(46)**

Hirschhorn's *World Airport* and *Bataille Monument* were process based but did not confront this issue of integration, however, his later *Cavemanman* is a centralised, birthing, gestating space for these issue of integration.

I think that the notion of the philistine is integral as whilst Enwezor and Bonami both call for the inclusion of marginal groups their religious character remains un-considered. The origin of the word Palestine is from Philistine **(47)** and I think that the Islamic faith in Palestine, and of other religious faiths, presents the last major "Philistinism" to challenge Western consumer culture. Interaction with these cultures might present a cultural montage that also has critical content.

The historical, progressive, criticality of Marxist Islam has been a seat of opposition to US commodity society but non-materialist commercial choices might also allow market forces to influence utopian thought, eg. Qiblah Cola as a drink started in Derby for Muslims who do not want to support American companies **(48)**.

I think that Hirschhorn sees dialectical thinking as failing to give Utopia. However as he remains within limited Western materialist critical and consumer perspectives he cannot entertain non-materialist consumer alternatives as a way to combine Benjamin's group myth (religion) with Adorno's call for an elite (critical) leadership to influence Spectacular society.

4 August 2003

Essay 7.

WHAT ARE THE POSSIBILITIES FOR POSTMODERN RELIGIOUS ART?

Introduction

There are a number of contemporary artists whose work could be described loosely as religious. This label is problematic for a number of reasons which I will spell out in this thesis.

Despite difficulties in defining the terms art, postmodernism and religion I suggest that there is an emerging trend that differs from all previous artistic expressions. The work making up this trend I name postmodern religious art. In order to keep the argument focussed I will refer to the work of four different artists to help illustrate the debates around this nebulous and cross-referential topic. Whilst every attempt is made to keep the references concrete there is an unavoidable amount of theory that must be included to give the intellectual context for the works under discussion.

The area covers debates in art, religion, theology, philosophy, social theory, sociology of religion and politics. I have tried to contextualise the works under discussion into some key areas of these debates but many areas have been left uncovered in order to construct a manageable argument. The analysis uses contemporary art theories that are mainly of a political nature, often with a spiritual underpinnings, as these provide the most relevant debates in art around this subject. I have tried to show how many examples of postmodern thinking are really modernist.

There is no assumption that the reader will believe in any of the religious arguments put forward. The sole purpose of these is hypothetical and as the argument progresses we will see how a hypothetical methodology used in religion can be an experimental expression of the artist.

First I will describe a collaboration of Damien Hirst and David Bailey, a performance by Guillermo Gomez Pena, the Plug 'n' Pray website and a website/performance by Shilpa Gupta. I will make a critical description, analysis, interpretation and evaluation of these works and will also use them to illustrate the progression of the argument.

After looking at the artists I will look at definitions of the different terms in postmodern religious art. I will point out that a feature of Modernism has been Utopian visions. I will then look at the oppositional strategy to this in deconstruction but argue that, in an extreme form, this has a mystical, utopian basis also. My solution is a weak form of utopianism and a weak form of nihilism. Both these weakened forms characterise postmodernism. Hirst represents the Nihilistic option and there are Marxist and consumer utopias – reflected by Gomez Pena and Shilpa Gupta respectively. Postmodern religious art involves a semi-ironic religious faith in bringing about a weak utopia that is consumerist rather than Marxist.

The Artists' Work

Damien Hirst and David Bailey's "The Stations of the Cross" exhibition at the Gagosian Gallery, London, April 30th – June 5th 2004 combined superficial fashion with deep religious issues but looked like a magazine shoot without any content or belief behind it.

The 150 cm x 100 cm prints were arranged in a white cube space and two white pillars in the middle of the room, which were part of the building, added to the churchlike feel of the work. There was no altar, pew or relic to pray to.

You enter the exhibition with a feeling of shock and oppression. You are confronted by images of skulls on ladies' legs, covered in blood, a cross covered in cigarette butts, a bloodied hand full of scalpels and a naked lady with a crown of thorns.

My initial reaction was that the work was brutal and aggressive. The domination and power of the corporate mediaeval church is mirrored in the domination of the corporate art world. The brutal materialism reinforced Hirst's faithlessness and made me cling to my own faith.

After seeing these four images my attention turned to the left wall where a severed cow's head lay in the knees of the lower half of a naked lady with shaven pubic hair. Feelings of sexual thrill, joined with revulsion and mocking were emphasised by a series of stylised and hollow glamour shots of models at the feet of a naked man (his head cut out of the photo frame) plus shots of David Bailey with Damien Hirst looking laughably and insincerely religious.

Barbed wire above a model's eye (VI) gave a heightened contrast between seeing life and the pain of death. Further contrasts were many women with one man (VIII) and a black model with a white man with whitened face and hair (IV). She smokes and the ash of her cigarette echoes the ash of his hair, also mirrored in the cigarettes stubbed out on the crucifix (XII).

The photographs are framed in wood that has been given a marbling effect (white with black veins) that echoes the barbed wire in the images. Inscribed in this, along the top, are symbols in gold lettering.

There is no clear order to how the works progress until you read the numbers on the frames. Stations IX – XII faced you, IV – VIII were on the left, II - III were behind and XIII, XIV & I were on the right. There is, however, a set of symbolic links between the works generated by repeated colour and imagery. The satanic colours of red, black, white and flesh tones are even echoed on a cardboard box tomb of Christ. The images mix blood, sharp metal (barbed wire and nails) and sexual perversion. The models' red blood and makeup echo each other in a satanic overtone where sex and death are linked with religion. The shaved female parts, and smooth, manicured models (nipples, lips and mascara) are echoed with the skulls. Bailey is the only clothed figure photographed, he is dressed in red robes, as Simon, and acts as an outsider called upon to help the naked Christ, here played by Hirst.

In XIII) "Taken down from the cross" there are two women, the black one holds the white one in an androgynous and multiracial Pieta. The identity of Jesus changes between man, woman, artist and model through the different works, suggesting that he/she is a universal figure. X) "Jesus is stripped" shows Jesus as the female model. Jesus is also "sanctified" as any gender in an erotic, lesbian style XIII, with its white, heavenly lit background. A sexual element is further cultivated with the adoring VIII) "Women of Jerusalem" around a naked man.

In contrast, a sense of butchered meat is given in the work. Human and cow skulls mix with fleshed out human and cow heads. The cows are also shown as freshly cut meat, carcasses and sausages – thus suggesting the same for the humans. Turning to the entry wall "Jesus carries his cross" (II) shows a black lady carrying a crucifix (a metal Jesus on the wooden cross) on a string of sausages. Christ as a temple sacrifice has been translated into a meat product to be purchased in a supermarket and religion is shown as a commodity to be bought and consumed.

This resemblance between cattle, sacrifice and human sacrifice is mocked. "Jesus falls for the first time" (III) is a severed cow's head with a skull covered in blood and a bowl of blood. VII) "Jesus falls the second time" is a cow's head, severed kneck fully exposed and IX) "Jesus falls the third time", is a skull shown with a comical jaw.

The mortality of humankind is further echoed by the reference to cigarettes, smoked by Christ's mother and stubbed out on the cross. "Jesus Meets his Mother" (IV) shows humans smoking "life enhancing" cigarettes but in XII) "Dies on the cross" stubbed out cigarettes rid the cross of holiness and reminds us that it was a base and ignoble way to die.

There is a sense of tenderness in VI) where "Veronica wipes the face of Jesus" as the model's vulnerable eye contrasts with the harsh barbed wire. There is also poignancy in XIV) "Jesus is Laid in the Tomb", a cardboard box with a white sheet to emphasise rubbishness and finality. Printed on the box are the ironic words "Caution – when lifting" and "Quality Office Products". Any pathos in the series is removed by comical puns and by self mocking such as V) "Simon helps Jesus" (Bailey helps Hirst).

Finally you come to I) "Jesus is Condemned to Die" which looks like an end image. Here sexuality, mortality, sacrifice and identity (not just between genders but between humanity, cattle and God) meet. The subject looks like a satanic figure already on a cross. It has a cow's skull crowned with barbed wire and has two carving knives raised, ready to stab. The work makes us question if the crucifixion was a satanic sacrifice of God, or a righteous one made by God. A morbid tone is set for the whole exhibition and there is no sense of a genuine religious sentiment, it is more mocking and destructive.

Is I) at the end of the exhibition, or at the beginning, or was it just easy to hang there as it is horizontal. The gallery assistant said that practical decisions prevailed. This further emphasises that the art gallery has taken over the religious space. The stations are hung as if in a sacred space but without any religious function.

Guillermo Gomez Pena's "Performance Lecture" for the 2004 "Fierce" Live Art Festival was in an old x-ray factory, on a run down industrial estate in West Birmingham. The audience had to queue outside the x-ray factory and then were let in according to classifications of illegal immigrants, blacks, south Asians, any Asians, women and finally men. These groups were let in one by one as a form of reverse discrimination. This allowed people to feel how it was to be discriminated for or against but felt to me like a game or an entertainment, rather than a serious challenge.

I went through into a medium sized, t-shaped room where, on a raised area, there was a body under an England flag, evoking ideas of a dead soldier returned from Iraq. At the head of this area was a blue lecturer's plinth. A smell of incense reminded me of the Church of the Holy Sepulchre in Jerusalem giving a Catholic, religious, pilgrimage feel to the event.

Even though the smell was spiritual the overall impression was of a sexual rather than spiritual nature. Images of previous performances were video projected onto a screen. These images included figures in semi-militaristic and sexually provocative clothing e.g. helmets, black balaclavas and short stockings, and with toy weapons. There were also images of naked figures on crucifixes in staged, red studio settings, being whipped or undergoing sado-masochistic sexual experiments. These images and accompanying religious music produced a confused sense of where you were and what you were looking at, that felt dark rather than uplifting.

Gomez Pena entered dressed in a knee length, dark skirt and women's high heels, with well-made upper body armour and a well-made, very large, bright red, plumed Indian head-dress. He had a goatee moustache and the aura of being a warrior/transvestite. He came in smelling of spirits and carrying a bottle.

A clinically dressed acupuncturist entered and needles were put into the person under the shroud. As he slowly pulled the shroud up you realised that underneath it was a woman. There were US flags on the needles that he began to put on the lower legs, then British further up the body and finally Israeli flags. He covered the naked body, working up from the torso and uncovering the breasts. The face was never revealed.

It felt that this was polemic against the US and symbolic of US colonialism over the planet or Iraq. With the flags the work seemed to be about the conquest of the feminine body but as acupuncture is a healing activity so the metaphor seemed unclear.

Gomez Pena began his lecture with loud and aggressive Mexican chanting. The work was theatrical but the aggression of the chanting made it more sincere. He took a mouthful of spirits and sprayed it over the body, from the podium, in a ritualistic and symbolic way. He then began the first part of his talk. His plinth and way of delivery was sermon-like but also funerary.

In his lecture he imagined how a mixture of Latin languages might sound and pointed out how the Anglo-American perspective is dominant even in language. He spoke of the first world being scared of ethnic minorities but how those minorities were both scared of the first world and of each other. He called for a healing of the nations and for people to unite to create change.

People were then asked to remove the flags. I was the second person to do this. I felt that I was doing something very tender and healing. The acupuncturist said to remove the flag slowly but I did it quite quickly and I was worried that I may have caused hurt. It was fine however. As other people took flags out it was like a decolonisation. People were asked to kiss the hands and feet of the body. When all the flags were removed then four pieces of incense were placed upon the body and lit. This increased the religious feel and Gomez Pena's chanting was a cross between politician, lecturer, shaman, Catholic priest or a surgeon. This reinforced the sense of healing or resurrection in a ritual where everyone was invited to join together.

The physicality and real pain are all part of the Catholic tradition of martydom. There was a strong religious feel but also a real bodily feel. Everyone applauded this strong performance and it left questions about whether it was just a symbolic or actually religious. There was a bizarre feeling that it was just a lecture but with a religious dimension that was sacrificial, coupled with a sexuality and a feeling of violent uprising.

Gomez Pena comes from a Latin American background of oppression for being a native and there is a recognition that change can come through violent struggle. He challenges violent oppression but wants to give a perspective on how a new politics might evolve. Blood and death, as well as religious symbols, highlight the creation of alternative identities as a strategy for overcoming oppression by challenging censors and allowing people to see new, liberating ways of behaving. The sexual element is also part of overcoming religious oppression as it challenges religious rules against homosexual and fetishistic acts.

The projected images (of a cross and sado-masochistic activity) blurred references to pleasure and pain, questioning what is good and bad for people. This was the same with the acupuncture mixed metaphor, in asking if it is healing or hurting. This created a confused space, but Gomez Pena was giving a definite political message with a strong religious overtone mixed with other tones.

Whilst the lecture had the appearance and smell of being religious I got the impression that it was too secular to have a strong religious force behind it. It was powerful but political and didn't have religious force. Religion was a part of the work, subsumed under politics, rather than being the main expression.

Gomez Pena is using, reinforcing and even glamourising, social stereotypes of sex and violence. There were religious aspects but everything was of an aggressive nature, linking to weaponry. He is almost trivialising prejudices and sexisms with his use of toy weaponry. Putting acupuncture needles in a woman is like the man penetrating the female and Gomez Pena is a man using a female artist (who was acknowledged in the performance but not credited in the literature) in a way that promotes his own work and ideas. This doesn't provide an alternative vision that is less sordid and less based in domination. No resolution is offered, just continued exploitation of these forms to make a point.

Political and social structures put people and ethnic groupings in a submissive role. Using extreme and powerful sexual, religious and racial imagery as a strategy to break free from dogmatism and religious oppression may be required but to be effective this needs mainstream media visibility and also runs the risk of alienating as many people as it encourages.

You enter Lionello Borean's "Plug 'n' Pray" website www.plug-pray.org and it has the image of a normal computer shop. A salesman in a suit and tie has religious symbols on his left side and on his right are colour coded computer boxes with symbols of various religions on their covers. The opening page has a trademark of the Holy Corporation and the statement "Getting converted has never been so easy." All the products are lined up like an educational resource and have the appearance of being professionally designed, with specifications stating that the product is easy to install, has manuals and has an online help system. The scene would be completely without irony apart from the title "START YOUR OWN HOLY WAR! Change their religion with "Plug 'n' Pray"". These add-ons for computers can be used to help in worship, but "their" (in the appeal to "change their religion") refers in an aggressive way to someone other than the purchaser.

When you click on "why do you need this", the idea is given that it is so that the user is able to change religion quickly to suit any social or political occasion. This is treating the religion as a lifestyle option. A critical point is implied, that the different religions all share the fact that they attach labels to themselves, almost like corporate branding. The boundary between a religion and a corporation is thus blurred and we can see elements of corporate branding in religion and of aggressive religious fervour in corporate marketing.

Details from Christian, Jewish and Muslim kits are advertised with Buddhist and Hindu options also available at a smaller size. They are advertised as having all the details of religious and cultural habits, fully illustrated in audio and visual files. The packs include cut out and wear cards to explain symbols and attires and the emphasis is on being able to customise the religion to meet your needs. The site continues with each religious symbol translated into a corporate identity of standard lime green logo and text on a white backdrop. This further standardises the religion as a commodity. The work appears to fully commodify religion in an electronic and Global age, but when you go to purchase the products you find that they are not available.

The site appears sincere but it has a mocking tone and promotes a concept of religious consumerism but not the application of a concept. It is not really promoting a religious alternative, just an ironic satire on that consumer alternative. Only the t-shirt competition is an actual application. Here artists around Europe have contributed t-shirt designs of how they see the Plug 'n' Pray concept. The contributions are mainly Christian and political but also include some other faiths and explore the relationship between sacred and secular life. The prize for the best works were voted for by the site visitors. In this way Plug 'n' Pray uses humour to criticise religious and corporate branding but also, hypocritically, promotes itself on t-shirts in the same way.

A deeper work is created by Shilpa Gupta. You enter her website, www.blessed-bandwidth.net, and see Hindu and Indian derived multi-religious imagery. On the site Gupta urges you to "get Blessed and Feel Secure", an ironic reference to the security of internet connections. As you move the mouse around the site a robed, monk-like figure carrying a rifle appears. The robes are combat camouflaged, suggesting a link between religion and military rule. You are also warned that you are being watched by the state but this appears as a playful, rather than a serious, statement.

You can "log on" and "immerse" yourself into the blessed bandwidth, implying a full experience, with gold and cerise circles giving feelings of heavenly peace. Four options are then given – "verification" "get blessed", "download" and "library". To enter each option you must choose from Hindu, Muslim, Sikh, Christian or Buddhist religions in Mumbai. A picture of the holy site comes up with a colourful image of architecture or deity from the religion in a band across the top of the screen, and information about its importance. Gupta then states that she took an Internet Network Cable and Requested blessings from various faith leaders, for peace and happiness, to whoever connects to the bandwidth of that cable.

To see images of how the cables are blessed and verified in different religions you are asked to comply with religious observances eg remove footwear, cover your head etc. Videos play of the actual ceremonies where you can see the full process of the cables being blessed by the priest or imam. In the process of verification you see rituals performed in a Hindu Temple, Muslim Mausoleum, Sikh Gurdwara, Chrisitian Church, Art of Living Holy Centre and a Buddhist Temple. There is a connection made between all the faiths by virtue of the same style of presentation of similar ritual processes for the blessing of the computer wires.

There is genuine and sincere reverence in this and whereas you may initially doubt the sincerity of the project this gives a feeling that a religious will was involved as the cable is blessed on each group's shrine. To believe the whole website is blessed as the very internet cable is blessed and that a blessing comes through the computer is an act of faith for the viewer to choose whether or not to make. In addition to this verification you can download a picture of the actual cable.

At the "Get Blessed" section the structure of the site was the same for each of the religions. I went to the Siddhivinayak temple first for blessing purely because it was the first on the list. The brightly coloured image of the Hindu elephant God, Ganesh, was in the centre in a circle with expanding coloured balls coming around it. There was a cross beneath his feet and the image zooms out and then back again. These effects, coupled with the Hindu imagery gives a kitsch feel for Western viewers and potentially removes the gravitas of the action. Hindu imagery is treated with sincerity and reverence in India but is often viewed as kitsch by Western standards. A western, global style would be more reflective of the cultural imperialism, homogeneity and commodification (that the is site warning us about) and less bias towards Hinduism. The other images in places for blessing that could be chosen were a Muslim shrouded figure of Sain Hajiali, the Gurdwara Shrine of Sikh Sri Dashmes Darbar, an image of Christ with sacred Heart, Sri Sri Ravi Shanka Guruji and an image of the Buddha.

Each image had the same coloured balls and step-by-step process for receiving a blessing. "1. Sit straight, don't lean. 2. Bend Slowly Forward. Concentrate. 3.Now touch your forehead to the computer screen on Spot X." I followed these instructions and then the computer pop-up said "would you like to certify the Blessing?" I clicked "OK" and then a download page to printout appeared with this text "this object has been blessed such that it will bring peace and happiness wherever it stands". You can even choose whatever border you would like for this printout. This downloads through the internet connection and when I picked up my printed page I felt a subjective connection to this being a religious object through all the rituals and rules I had followed on how to approach the blessing. I felt that it was also an interreligious object because of the connection to other faiths. I was not convinced that anything religious had occurred but had a small sense that something of meaning and significance might have occurred.

Gupta's materials are the rituals of religions and so her work is meta-religious because it in not directly religious itself. It is a structure that organises different religions and a connection between communities was made. The connection is not radical as you choose religions and forms of worship that are still very traditional, just put into an internet context.

A radical form of worship is in one of her various downloads on the site. "God.exe" is a small pop-up on the screen. It is like a children's computerised pet "tamagochi" toy that you can electronically love, feed and pray to it. The image that comes up is a yellow eye with a black iris. It has cerise eyelids on a yellow, vertical oval, itself on a cerise, horizontal oval with a yellow, vertical oval band behind this. On the cerise oval are peaceful symbols, as well as symbols from different religions. The eye symbolism is universal and neutral - although the style of this is Hindu and not really interfaith. By feeding sugar, milk and fruit to "God" we act like a child with a toy or like someone who is worshipping an idol. There is a sense that is just frivolous but this gets to the crux of the work. Is there any reality to this God? The work is strong for allowing this to be left for the viewer to decide.

A weakness with "God.exe" (and the site as a whole) is that Gupta promotes looseness and individual creativity, not restrictions, yet there is too much certainty and strictness about her structure. In "God.exe" there is an allocation of times for reverence, love, quiet, excitement and stillness. By adhering to these times and by choosing to offer different kind of love (endless, natural, diminishing, not sure) you are appealing to Gupta's God, not a universal God. I felt that she has not the authority to create this God and we are not given the tools to construct it ourselves. The request to say a prayer is the most genuine aspect. You are invited to stare at an image and to say a prayer, which I did to help me progress, love people and do what is right. Then the machine adds a prayer against right wing governments in a further example of Gupta's control.

A much freer piece is in the "Library" section. In the "Closet" you can click and drag items from different religions onto a figure and dress it up in a variety of ways. The unisex cartoon figure is naked and you can select from headdresses, headscarves, turbans and a crown of thorns. You can select robes, leg-wear, trousers, loincloths, boots, sandals and shoes of Hindus, Muslims and Christians. You are also able to hold guns, bibles, prayer rattles and candles. This exercise is radical and fun but has no real connection to any real possibilities in life or worship. There is not the religious connection or authenticity in this work. It is just a child's play experience, like velcro strips in a primary school dressing pad and is too divorced from real action or fashion.

Definitions of Religion

To understand if these works are "Postmodern Religious Art" I will look at a number of definitions of the term's constituent parts then relate the work of the artists to the various definitions. Whilst religion can be given a definition the terms art and postmodernity are almost defined as having no clear definition. To begin with I will look at definitions of religion. These are often off-set against definitions of spirituality.

The term religion is concerned with immanence, outward forms of doctrine, faith, behaviour and worship. The term spirituality is concerned with transcendence, inward, meditation experiences and personal experiences that are often inarticulable.

In his influential 1902 Gifford lectures at Edinburgh University in *The Varieties of Religious Experience* William James states this division. "At the outset we are struck by one great partition which divides the religious field. On the one side of it lies institutional, on the other personal religion". Worship, sacrifice, theology, ceremony and ecclesiastical organisation are on the institutional side and inner dispositions, conscience, desires and incompleteness are on the personal. The personal relation is direct, heart to heart and soul to soul between man and his maker.

He continues "in these lectures I propose to ignore the institutional branch entirely, to say nothing of the ecclesiastical organisation, to consider as little as possible the systematic theology and ideas about the gods themselves, and to confine myself as far as I can to personal religion pure and simple." **(1)**

James is more in favour of the spiritual approach – as, I shall argue, are most modern artists. However, I propose that a postmodern religious approach has a focus on the gods and institutional, outer forms that James 'ignores' and 'considers as little as possible'.

The above works all share symbolism used in various religious traditions yet they no longer have a sense of following a single belief structure or iconography as in earlier forms of religious art such as

Michaelangelo's "Pieta" or the carving in Gothic Cathedrals. Hirst uses Christian symbolism, Gomez Pena combines Christian and South American Indian shamanistic symbolism whilst Gupta and Plug'n'Pray expand use to symbols from various religions. The symbols are removed from their original context and used as art that no longer serves religion and now serves itself or other causes. Hirst and Bailey's work is a high fashion commodity (published in the fashion magazine "Another Magazine"), Gomez Pena's work is political and the internet based works of both Plug'n'Pray and Gupta mimick more general consumer items.

Religion is often defined as requiring a large following eg Christianity, Islam, with smaller or more recent groups being called "cults", "sects" and "new religious movements" eg Scientology, Sufism. In my investigation I will look at belief systems that are called religions and ones that are called cults. I cover both as post-enlightenment artistic expression is often individual, (rather than institutional, large or widespread,) yet can still be religious in nature. I will not make any assumptions about the relative validity or veracity of religious claims just how they relate to the postmodern art under discussion.

Definitions of Art

Next I will look at definitions of art and how the above works might become classified as art. James Elkins presents a social definition, Cynthia Freeland examines the roles of aesthetics and meaning and Marc C. Taylor (one of the few theorists combining an analysis of religion, art and philosophy) presents a history of how an aesthetic view came to dominate art discourse. I argue that, since Immanuel Kant (1724-1804), art theorists have preferred aesthetic expression (over meaningful content) as a way to reunite the domains but that postmodern religious art theorists should prefer meaningful content.

James Elkins is sympathetic to religious art and has investigated the fate of religion in contemporary art. In his definitions he thinks that what is classed as art is so varied that almost anything can be included within the term. His social definition of the term is work that is produced by artists, exhibited in galleries or published in art magazines **(2)**. This means many popular objects of a religious or artistic nature are excluded.

On this definition Hirst is fully within art circles, so his work is art, but Cynthia Freeland attempts a non-social definition which explains why he might be allowed into those circles. Freeland sees great variety and a freedom for any message to be contained within a work of art but she identifies two strands of art, those containing expression and those containing content **(3)**. She sees artwork like Hirst's as having elements of both ritualistic content and artistic expression. It is representational of blood ritual but is not the sacrificial ritual of a religion nor is it purely beautiful or aesthetic like a Romantic conception of art.

Marc C. Taylor thinks that the Romantic conception has dominated modern art discourse and that pivotal to understanding the romantic conception of art is the philosophy of Immanuel Kant. Taylor describes Kant's philosophy of aesthetics in the *Critique of Pure Reason* **(4)**. Kant tried to discover a connection between the way our minds interpret the world with the world itself. The information that we collect through our various senses, is translated into understandable experiences that are ordered by universal processes of reasoning. The mode by which we pass from this personal sense data to an understanding of the data is, for Kant, via the imagination in an act of synthesis. This synthesis is fundamental to our experience and lies behind all our thought processes.

An experience of beauty is seen as the bridge between understanding and the external world. The beautiful form presented in the sense data finds accord with the beautiful structure of reason and thus the properties exist both internally and externally. This aesthetic sense unites internal and external domains but is replaced with a sublime fear and dread when the very possibility of being able to unite these domains is broken down. The sublime is the sense when an experience or object is present to thought yet also exceeds all thought. The mind is unable to conceive of the size or force of an experience and the inadequacy of the understanding is felt in face of the vast and dreadful open possibility of the imagination.

Two early nineteenth century philosophers who tried to fill, rather than combat, the space generated by an experience of the sublime, were F.W.J. Schelling and G.W.F. Hegel. Schelling proposed a link between the internal and external by joining of internal and external in an intellectual intuition that the individual is identical with absolute being. All difference is removed by intuiting that the one is the many and that subject becomes object. This absolute being was seen as a pantheistic, spiritual, mystical identity with the whole universe. In contrast to this intuition Hegel proposed a joining of subject and object in an intellectual reasoning. This system, based on rational argument rather than on intuition, showed a historical progression to the idea of the individual as identical with absolute being. Difference is removed within a total system/structure created by dialectical reasoning **(5)**. It is this search for a unity that characterises Modernism, with uniting opposites in art either representing an intellectual system of thought, like Hegel's philosophy, or a direct experience, like Schelling's philosophy.

Works, like those of Gomez Pena or Gupta, can attempt to provide solutions with political and social structures that are used to combat a sense of sublime dread. Faith in progress and faith in God give hope that fear and dread at nature's sublime forces can be overcome. Beauty can also enhance these strategies and is used in representations of progression by science and politics. As I will describe later, postmodernism differs in that belief in progress is semi-ironic.

Hirst's work rejects the sense of dread and creates a sense of breaking out of aesthetic structures. Freeland argues that Hirst's art breaks away from a purely aesthetic or expressive criteria for evaluating art to one that is also based on meanings or content **(6)**. Hirst directly referenced the sublime in his previous exhibition at the White Cube 2003 "Romance in the Age of Uncertainty". His horrific exhibition of severed cows heads is a parody of the sublime. Any sense of awe is diffused in a sense of melodrama and schlock horror. The "aura" of the art object is deflated away from depth of experience to being a superficial statement that mocks the impossibility of finding an absolute connection between art and life.

The religious power of Hirst's work came from both the institutional display and the work itself. The power of the art commodity institution is like a religious institution. This threatens to engulf the individual but is not sublime, it is political. The carnal nature of his work reinforced the gallery's metaphorical ability to perform sacrifices in order to transform base materials into money. This seemingly unstoppable marketing machine is a human creation that opposes sublime dread but by schlock horror and humour, instead of religious faith.

Hirst's work rejects a need for traditional/"natural" notions of beauty and aesthetics. It is an oppositional aesthetic (ie ugly posing as beautiful) and not a positive alternative to overcome a sense of dread.

Definitions of Modernism

Before we look at how people with views favouring spiritual intuition influenced modern art and how dialectical reasoning affected modernist politics we will look at definitions of Modernism, Modernity or Modernisation. Modernisation, usually means to bring things up to date with what is the most efficient and latest object or process, Modernity is another name for the modern age which is the result of modernisation and Modernism is the set of underlying assumptions involved in following Modernity.

There are multiple definitions and perspectives on what is Modernism but the most obvious relates to science and technology. Modernism often involved a search for universal answers, formal qualities and definitions in a "Grand Narrative" of progress. There was optimism about science, urbanisation, industrialisation and reason in attempts to understand the self and the world (and overcome sublime dread). People claimed that science needed no justifying as it progressed towards a complete knowledge, united in common goals and methods and of benefit to humanity. After people experienced the mechanised horrors of the second world war these myths collapsed and the creation of weapons of mass destruction and ecological disasters has further undermined belief in modern progress.

Whilst an anglo-american philosophical (empiricist's or logical positivist's) view of science, art and religion would be interesting to the debate I am restricting an analysis of modernity to issues arising from continental philosophy, as I have found these to have the most influence on contemporary art practice and theory. To begin with I make passing reference to the philosophy of science developed by Jean-Francois Lyotard.

In "The Postmodern Condition" Lyotard looked at the development of scientific and hypothetical thinking. He argued that what is regarded as scientific objectivity changes depending on social and cultural conditions. Knowledge is limited by the institutions and the rules they operate within. The truths and universal values that bind a society or ideology together are really just meta-narratives which claim to be objective about other forms of knowledge (7).

The postmodern artist is critical of scientific and technological assumptions but is also immersed within them, in a potentially hypocritical relationship. Gomez Pena uses technological weaponry, but in order to criticise oppressive rulers. His work intimates a threat that oppressed people will launch an uprising and use this technology against the oppressors. The weapons were toys and the exhibition was too theatrical and superficial to carry the weight of a concept of sexual and violent politics. Gupta uses technology more directly and shares the modernist interest in technology being used to help create world peace and bring a universal harmony. But within her work the hooded, military figure shows an awareness that this is also a medium of surveillance and control. Despite this worry she has a position of hope and optimism that comes from a semi-ironic religious faith.

In contrast to the above Hirst's dissected bodies can be seen as postmodern, nightmare experiments gone wrong or as a scientific or medical investigation into materials - under the surgeon/butcher's knife. There is more of a glorification of science's total control of society than an attempt to overcome the threat of such control. Similarly Plug "n" Pray is fully complicit with technology and consumer control with its packages to change/improve behaviour patterns.

I will address postmodern complicity between art, questionable technology and commodity later. First I will look at another Grand Narrative, the modernist political analyses of cultural and artistic production.

This political thought relates mass media images to issues of Karl Marx's analysis of an oppressive "cultural superstructure". This line of thinking has been developed by Benjamin, Adorno, Horkheimer, Greenberg and Debord from the potentially positive effects of the mass media on critical thinking to its complete pacifying of the political imagination and ability to see reality. Baudrillard takes this latter view to a postmodern conclusion, arguing that we are completely engulfed in an inescapable viewpoint that separates the individual from political reality by an alienating superstructure

Marx (1818-1883) developed Hegel's dialectical thinking into a secular system which influenced many art theorists. Glenn Ward describes how Marx saw that, in an industrial, Capitalist system, for people to be able to buy commodities, they need to sell their labour and become a commodity themselves. The workers are alienated from the objects that they produce and do not have a role in a more communal form of life. Money becomes the new social bond and society is based on "exchange values" rather than "use values". When "exchange value" (money) is less than should be given for the "use value" (work done) exploitation results **(8)**.

Society was seen as having two levels, an "economic base" of commercial realities and a "cultural superstructure" of the entertainment and politics that function on top of this. The superstructure produces goods for people to fill the gap in their lives that the economic exploitation creates. These goods are designed so that you cannot see that they are created by a system whose inadequacy creates the need for them in the first place. Marx wanted the worker to see this relationship to the capitalist system through a critical analysis that proposed progression to reach an end of exploitation and to create a united, communist society based on equality.

In "The Work of Art in the age of Mechanical Reproduction" 1936, Walter Benjamin argued that technologies of mass production could make art equally available to everyone. Original works were given an "aura" of exclusivity that could be stripped away by making mass copies. Cinema in particular became the example of a mass art that did not even have a single, original copy. Older works of art often had special powers because of their use within religious cults and ceremonies and Benjamin thought it was good to strip away that aura and allow open access to all people **(9)** however he was unsure that this would be responsibly handled.

The problem for him was that mass production gave more items at a faster rate and thus it was hard to be critical about all of these. Critical thinking requires concentration and Benjamin thought that the masses received work as a form of distraction, rather than thoughtfully. "the public is an examiner, but an absent minded one" **(10)**. Fascist and capitalist production without critical thought allows exploitative politics to be represented as an aesthetic form to promote and glorify war. **(11)** This theorising occurred in the context of the growth of fascist mass spectacles, Soviet social realism and an increasingly commercialised mass culture.

In "Dream World of Mass Culture" Susan Buck-Morss says that Benjamin proposed that the world of images produced by consumer society has a limited life and is continually replaced by newer fashions and images. This constant change opens up the possibility of a radical reconstruction of the fragmented reality of industrial society. Such reconstruction lies at an unconscious, mythic, level in human beings. **(12)** Benjamin **(13)** states that a waking being is aware of its concrete historical situation by placing itself in a politically empowered, critical, dialectical ideology of progress.

Whilst Benjamin thought that mass culture had a critical potential Theodor Adorno and Max Horkheimer, in "The Culture Industry" 1945, described mass culture as being empty stylisation that involves cheap parody and not the transcendent asceticism of high culture. They also questioned whether technology and reproduction would lead to a more critical, popular art. Adorno thought that low culture creates individuals who seek identity by imitating manufactured capitalist stars and uses humour to promote resignation to oppressed conditions. Thus, only dialectical, critical, thinking can give alternatives to popular culture. Adorno's view is that critical (dialectical) leadership/culture should be given to people and that it should not be influenced by popular culture **(14)**.

Aspects of Clement Greenberg's early work parallel Adorno's and both made a distincition between high art and popular culture in modern capitalist societies. Greenberg argued, in his influential 1939 essay Avant-Garde and Kitsch, that the Avant-Garde was needed to stop culture going into the hands of capitalism and fascism. He argued that the avant-garde was concerned with innovation and progress but fascist countries used kitsch in order to keep them connected with the masses and as a way to revere past-masters and historical culture. Much of the mass produced advertising and imagery is what Clement Greenberg termed kitsch. This is work that was produced to directly appeal to popular taste and is usually representational rather than abstract, often relating to national ideals and idylls. True socialism would give the right conditions for education so that people can appreciate true (ie. avant-garde and abstract) culture **(15)**.

The danger of social control through using shallow imagery, was theorized by Guy Debord in an idea called the Spectacle. This Spectacle of images is used to ensnare people and the rejection of this social control influenced the radical student movements of the 60's. In his book on "Guy Debord" Anselm Tappe says that the Spectacle is conceived of as an ensemble of independent, commodity representations. The spectator is separate from these images and is an isolated individual **(16)**. In "The Society of the Spectacle" 1967 Guy Debord argued that the economy of late 20th century society is driven by images. Production and consumption of commodities is so prevalent that life is now lived around images of these commodities. Our experiences and relationships become packaged and commodified for us. We watch our experiences rather than have them for ourselves and become apathetic about thinking that we can change how we should feel. The spectacular society tries to deny a view of history as being part of a dialectical progression **(17)**. Debord thinks that opposition to the Spectacle is by dialectical (critical) thinking and by having personal relations based around direct communication between people, not consumer activities **(18)**. The "Situationist International" movement arose out of this opposition to the Spectacle and members tried to create events and experiences that broke out of packaged and commodified ways of thinking.

In response to their feelings of being trapped within a commodity system, some individual artists acknowledged, and worked with, their complicity with this political structure. This can be seen in the work of Andy Warhol, who took mechanical means of reproduction and applied them to imagery from popular culture and advertising in work that was flat and with brash colours. There are numerous interpretations of Warhol's work, and this political interpretations is just one of these.

In his survey, of the American avant-garde since 1970, Henry. M. Sayre, Associate Professor of art at Oregon University states how Andy Warhol's "Maos" 1974 and "Hammer and Sickles" 1976 gave an empty reminder of how the political nature of art could be turned into commodity (even as "Mao Wallpaper"). Warhol thought that even the avant-garde had become a marketable notion so artists must accept their market status to attempt to overcome it **(19).** In his paper for the 1985 ICA conference on Postmodernism Michael Newman questions how far Warhol was overcoming pop culture through deconstructing it, as even deconstruction can be seen as complicit, careerist opportunism on the part of the artist **(20).**

Similiarly, does Warhol express religious devotion or lack of devotion in mass produced Catholic images like "The Last Supper" series 1986. Warhol's presentation of the divine, or perfectly packaged, body is contrasted with Hirst's brutal and pseudo-scientific presentation of this body. Hirst's presentation of Catholic-style stations of the cross is severed cows heads, whilst Warhol's presentation is kitsch/idealistic Catholic art, but both are marketing tactics complicit with consumerism.

The impossibility of breaking out of the Spectacle is theorised by Baudrillard **(21).** It is this breakdown of certainty in the idea of progress that informs the theory and artworks of postmodernism. Baudrillard argued that when we approach places/objects/people our minds are already full of preconceptions given to us by media images of those places/objects/people. Brand names, cinematic stereotypes, music videos etc, are complete fantasy and when a work is produced as a mass produced object, without original copy, then a level of deception is begun as the simulation of an original object becomes the real object.

However, although these images no longer have "auras" as original objects in the real world, the system of simulations has become so widespread that there is no reality outside of this system. Society has constructed itself out of myths that have taken on a role that is more important than actual reality and as such are a "hyperreality". In this way we have no experience that is not simulated. It becomes impossible to see the difference between natural and manufactured desires.

Baudrillard's ideas apply particularly with reference to computer imagery and the internet. Borean's Plug 'n' Pray shows that this hyperreality is more important than the actual reality as none of his works are actual products. Gupta's work is complicit with hyperreality by suggesting that to worship on-line is just as fulfilling as worshipping in a real location. This religion is simulation as it takes images of images of religion and mixes them in commodified pictures of reality.

Baudrillard did not think that the simulated world was a deliberate process to keep people oppressed but rather he thinks that a society requires signs, codes and simulations to function. To escape simulation people may try to follow something that makes them feel that they are connecting back to something real but he thought that nothing can actually take people out of media simulations.

Making disturbing art could be a strategy to shock people out of simulations but even gruesome, dissected cows have become a trademark for Damien Hirst. Using these dissected cows as religious signs Hirst and Bailey exploit the shock value of their work, as if it related to real life, but really just reinforce the importance of themselves and their superficial image system. Gomez Pena's work offers shock as a political alternative by taking images from mass media and combines them in ways that question their power and control over the individual but he uses toy weapons. Alternative models of freedom are also provided in Gupta's work, but this is less militant and has direct connotations of commodity and quick consumerism. Nevertheless, consciousness may be raised by shocking and new artworks and I will now look at whether these can lead to the creation of a group or political movement with any power.

Postmodern Online Communities?

Ideas about the spectacle and "hyperreality" developed a body of theory on how community effort can oppose these oppressive constructs. Marshall McLuhan argues that the structure of new technology might provide a way to do this.   McLuhan was influential on Baudrillard and wrote on how he believed that the media revolution had led to a decentralising of the world into virtual communities and that the structure of computing meant more for social and psychological change than its contents.   The structure leads to a high degree of audience participation and non-linear thinking that can bring communities around the world together. Ward points out that this community remains largely Euro-American as only Westerners can afford the technology. Community interaction is also not necessarily harmonious, with the media used by competing multi-national corporations and different political and religious factions **(22)**.

Gupta's work reflects a degree of suspicion about the structure of the internet being used for control over religious freedoms. You are informed not to panic but that you are being watched from an I.P. address and this gives a level of pretend suspicion and paranoia underlying contemporary attitudes towards religion. The work, however, also excludes many people that it tries to connect with, as the high memory using "Flash" programme is needed to enter the site.

Ward discusses Mark Poster's argument that as national borders dissolve, and new ways to communicate are introduced, so also central authority dissolves and the private consumer becomes simultaneously the public producer. The internet provides new ways for communities to form and these virtual, on-line communities can be used politically **(23)**. However, these virtual communities, that Poster describes, may develop bonds between individual consumer groups but Ward thinks that a diversification of consumer groups can lead to less centralised, politically weaker, challenges to abuses of power **(24)**.

This homogenisation and control of the internet and telecommunications is another example of why modernist technological progress might not provide the political strategy to overcome centralised abuses of power.

Both Gupta and Borean initiate communities by allowing people to participate and have notes or comments. But there is no real direction or political intent produced. In the "Photo album", in Gupta's "Library", there are images that people have uploaded from around the world. You must enter your name, what God does for you, an image and a name with description for the images. This makes an online community that is superficial but is also fun and friendly. Examples are mainly Hindu, from India, and what God does is show people the way or helps them pass exams. The other choice in the library is the Rules Desk, which allows the viewer to submit a rule they like and one they don't. Examples range from Zarin who says "I love to dress up for festivals" but "can't keep up with fasting" to Suzy who says "I love to pray before having food" but "Had 5 abortions till now". This last rule contains a shocking confession and only here is there is a sense that something can progress in the debate, rather than this just being a fun website.

A spiritual dimension can be ascribed to the internet as the connections exist in an immaterial space and over vast distances. I will not look into the vast debate of the implications of this for postmodern religious art as the internet is perhaps more a spiritual sphere, with downloads as the concrete, religious manifestations. I will look at spiritual strategies after investigation postmodern multiculturalism.

Postmodern Multiculturalism?

Another strategy for overcoming oppressive structures is multiculturalism, but there are arguments for and against its effectiveness. At first the link with internet, interactive technology may seem tenuous but artists like Gupta use technology to try like communities and overcome oppressive structures and multiculturalism uses theoretical strategies to do the same. This section looks at how Okuwi Enwezor argues that in a postmodern context community opposition needs to be multicultural but Patrice Pavis is concerned that it is possible that this can be an oppressive appropriation by dominant ideologies. Erika Doss then describes how minority artist Gomez Pena mixes identities to critique dominant ideologies.

In his introduction to "Documenta XI" Okuwi Enwezor called for a more inclusive and global art that addressed marginalized ethnic groups and viewed Ground Zero metaphorically, as a new starting point and a space for cultures other than those of the USA to grow and engage in debate. With media focus on a "clash of civilisations" the marginalized culture of Islam has now become a focus of attention. The dead certainties of colonialism and modernism have come to a crisis point and Enwezor believes that Muslim culture is contesting this space. He does not think that a radical form of Islam will gain support from other global, cultural groups, (or anti-globalisation groups) but he thinks that interaction with marginal cultures in a montage has critical content and presents the last major challenge to Western consumer culture **(25)**.

Patrice Pavis, the editor of <u>The Intercultural Performance Reader</u>, worries that interculturalism is just an appropriation of other cultures by a dominant culture that will destroy the cultures which it assimilates. The appearance of a global culture is not democratic but is really the subsuming of all individual cultures under the dominant West (consumerism) **(26)**. This view is backed up by the work studied. Borean looks at many religious cultures but they are all united in consumerism. Gupta's work is more nuanced but it is still controlled as she looks at many religious cultures through the structure of her website, rather than through commodity. Only Gomez Pena's work has radical, free mixing.

Erika Doss writes about Gomez Pena's work in her study of Twentieth-Century American art. She says that he explored how ethnic identities are constructed as scientific curiosities and how they are also commodified as stereotypes for media consumption. Doss says that Gomez Pena thinks that multicultural pluralism cannot counter dominant cultural perspectives, as cultural forms are appropriated but no control is given back to the other cultures. His suggestion is to use a syncretic model where identities are not sharply defined and are used as a way of critiquing political authority and social oppression **(27)**.

Gomez Pena describes some of his ideas of such a syncretic model in *Dangerous Border Crossers: the artist talks back* . His mission is "to create new, hybrid ritual capable of expressing our fears and contradictions, or existential malaise, our political uncertainties and trans- or inter-cultural complexities **(28)**." These hybrid identities are a combination of parts but have no fixed essence. The hybrid personas that he creates eg: pregnant nuns, holy gang members, crucified political activists, curio shop shamans, and pop cultural madonnas appear to be religious/(anti)religious. Examples of these hybrids are collected on his website.

Despite Gomez Pena's optimism hybrids like these could easily fit what Michael Newman describes as the postmodern movement called the Trans-avantgarde. This work is without avant-garde political intention other than to confuse symbolic expectations and break-down historical imagery. Newman points out that whilst the avant-garde had specific political purposes the transavant-garde just wish to break down of rationality **(29)**.

Bonito Oliva and Frederick Jameson are theorists who argue that a superficial mixing of cultures has no political role and creates a depthless society. On the political effects of art Bonito Oliva proposed that art now operates like a game without political challenge. He proposed that the historic avant-garde was involved in a critical, dialectical progression of reuniting opposites but in contrast to this the Trans-avantgarde, founded in Italy in 1979, rejected ideological progress, preferring to imitate and fragment various historical art forms. Instead of a expressing a grand avant-garde synthesis, artists such as Sandro Chia, Francesco Clemente, Enzo Cucchi and Mimmo Paladino just made an eclectic use of diverse imagery. Figurative elements are joined with abstract elements, and historical art images are linked with popular culture but the appropriation is ironic, liminal, without cohesion, synthesis or political direction and is just another marketable commodity **(30)**.

The American Marxist critic Frederick Jameson in "Postmodernism, or the Cultural Logic of Late Capitalism" considers that art and popular culture have collapsed into each other and as such art no longer has a role in providing any criticism of society. It has become just a form of advertising and is mechanically produced. The superficial effect is all that is important and the depth is lost. Signs that used to have meaning are taken and used as pastiche combinations of various styles and as a form of mocking parody.

Jameson argues that multinational media and communications corporations control global economics and that individuals and nations are divided into specialised consumer groups with no real collective power. The overarching power in the world is "late capitalism" and cultural, historical and geographical difference are losing importance. People are surrounded and charmed by a mass of "overstimulating" experiences that have no real depth **(31)**. Gomez Pena's hybrids seem to be just one more example of these experiences.

Postmodernism is a recognition of the failed optimism of Grand Narratives such as science and politics. Whilst Gomez Pena may be optimistic that his art can have a political effect it is postmodern if he recognises that it probably will not or if he is semi ironic in intent. Our final source of optimism in modernism is spirituality.

Modernist Spiritual Utopias

A rejection of superficial and ineffectual art could come from what Freeland describes as a deeper spiritual link between cultures. However, even the art rituals and ceremonial objects from Indians, Chinese, Hindu and Muslim groups, can often be purchased as commodities and Freeland describes "primitive", "authentic" and "exotic" cultures as religions under the condition of Late Modernity. Indigenous art has also been affected by contact with Western techniques of production. **(32)**

Freeland describes an exhibition in 1989 called "Les Magiciens de la Terre" at the Pompidous Centre for Modern Art where the earthworks installation piece ,"Red Earth Circle," by Richard Long was exhibited above an earth painting by a collective of Yuendumu

Aborigine artist. The precise description of this work is not as important as the response of Freeland "It is hard to deny that there is a hint of New Age spiritualism in the show's title, which smacks of the desire for "authentic" spirituality and shamanistic authority, to escape participation in a crass and demeaning art market system. (33)" I argue that such "New Age" spirituality is essentially modernist and is a unity resembling Schelling's intellectual intuition (and Hegel's dialectical reasoning). In contrast, it is precisely the commercialism (and not spirituality) which postmodern religious art would include.

This spiritualism is a popular view that arose from Theosophical doctrines concerning the need to balance opposites in a united, transcendent consciousness. Taylor believes that this is as if Hegel's ideas were put into a populist spiritual context **(34)**. John Golding, painter, curator and art historian, argues that Piet Mondrian is just one of many artists influenced by Hegel's dialectic (with his view that art was a way towards God) and by Madame Helena Petrovna Blavatsky's Theosophical theories (from the late nineteenth century), that evolution occurs through the balancing of opposites in a continually changing process **(35)**. Blavatsky's view that fluidity and water are the fundamental reality shows in the visual rhythm, throb and dynamism of Mondrian's work **(36)**.

Golding thinks that flat, abstract art is more truthful than illusionism on a painted surface, so flatness can be used in order to bring spiritual truth near to the viewer. As a result Mondrian intends his painting's surface to become the whole image – and not to just contain representations within the painting's surface **(37)**. Eg "Composition with Yellow, Red, Black, Blue and Grey", oil on canvas, 1920.

Clement Greenberg argued for an art form with a beauty that is both in the understanding and in the object. Painting was isolated from other arts, as an activity in itself which was an investigation of the formal properties of paint. What was particular to the medium was flatness, as this was the property of the canvas, and abstraction **(38)**. Mark Rothko engaged in this investigation but also linked ideas of spirituality and a sublime expression beyond the purely formal in his artworks **(39)**. He engulfed his viewers in his dark, profound colour paintings eg "No.10", 1950, Oil on canvas, 1950. These acted like doorways to the infinite, passing through a dividing line that is like the horizon point of landscape **(40)**.

The works of Mondrian and Rothko take many sources for their inspiration, eg. notions of scientific progress and psychological understanding of the individual consciousness. Spirituality is just the one we are considering at present. Unfortunately the spiritual changes associated with transcendent realities and links to a unity beyond the world are too abstract for the majority of people and so have had little mass political effect.

This focus on a transcendent spiritualism is often characterised as modernist with the mass consumerism of Pop art often characterised as postmodern. Taylor sees Pop art as modernist postmodernism and not postmodernism proper. He argues that even consumerism holds a modernist promise of a united utopia of consumer salvation **(41)** whereas postmodernism proper denies all unity and utopias. For Taylor the unity sought in Modernism can be outside the world (transcendent and spiritual) or fully within it (immanent) whereas in postmodernism neither is possible as there are irreconcilable divisions and disunities in reality. **(42)** Before looking critically at this idea I will describe the idea of utopian modernism to evaluate whether it holds any critical hope.

Interviewed for the catalogue of the 50th Venice Biennale (2003) Immanueal Wallerstein (author of "Utopistics") stated that the term Utopia was invented by Sir Thomas More in the 16th century and means "nowhere" in Greek. He said that a Utopia is seen as being an impossible place and an act of imagination concerning what a good society should look like **(43)**.

All of the other works under discussion (other than Hirst's) can be seen as pointing to a positive progression and a desire for Utopian change. Plug 'n' Pray, however, is ironic in its description of the Utopian value of religious products and so does not offer a genuine solution. The works of Gomez Pena and Gupta offer solutions but from different bases, from a deep and revolutionary opposition to consumerism and from a complicity with superficial consumerism respectively.

Taylor views spirituality and consumerism as two stems from the same absolutist, Utopian root. Critical and consumer utopias, involve critical rejection or complicity with the market respectively. An attempt to overcome the difference between market opposition and complicity in "modernist postmodernism" is given by David Harvey, who calls for a regulation of consumerism with critical thinking, and John Roberts, who needs clearer critical regulation.

In "Spaces of Hope" David Harvey makes this difference between a temporal (critical, dialectical Marxist) versus a spatial (free-market, neo-liberal, capitalist) utopian space. He sees these as potentially united but doesn't want a closed capitalist system. Rather he wants the innovative change associated with capitalist experimentation to apply to the system as a whole. **(44)** Harvey suggest a consumerist cultural relativism regulated by a critical, Marxist, basis. John Roberts in "Philosophies of the Everyday" proposed that cultural relativism gives a cultural montage that has little political effect. Although the montages can give rise to counter cultures these counter cultures are absorbed as consumerist counter cultures separate from critical and emancipatory histories. **(45)** Thus dialectical regulations are required by Roberts. This just seems to be a restatement of Benjamin's and Adorno's positions mentioned earlier and no new method to bring about these critical regulations is described. This apparent impasse between critical and consumer utopian thinking is unnecessary for Taylor.

Postmodern Non-Utopias?

Taylor argues that modern aesthetics began around the idea of Kant's sublime but that instead of searching for a fundamental, aesthetic unity, an alternative is postmodernism. This is characterised by a more radical, completely divided and non-utopian stance **(46)**. This fits with psychological models, such as Jean-Francois Lyotard's, based around a divided self, rather than an indivisible individual. I shall describe below how Jacques Derrida also applies this notion to deconstructing institutions and discourses and how Julia Kristeva characterises this in the arena of sexuality as a feminine response to rigid male systems. Taylor argues that true postmodernism is a breakdown of all fixed perspectives but I will argue how a radical breakdown takes us back to a modernist position **(47)** so postmodernism should be characterised as less extreme, or semi-ironic, about possibilities of utopia.

Postmodernists do not ascribe to a single definition or viewpoint but many think that Modernist regulations and institutions repress and control the self. This self is divided by many postmodernists who see people as having no fixed identity but rather as having multiple selves. Lyotard argues that the self is made of irreconcilable parts and that society (or culture) itself is made of aspects that cannot be united **(48)**.

Similarly, Poststructuralists, such as Jacques Derrida, reject any claim for underlying, formal meaning. Such single meanings are seen as totalitarian and imperialist by poststructuralists. Structuralists, such as the anthropologist Claude Levi-Strauss and the psychoanalyst Jacques Lacan, thought that systems of meaning were relatively fixed and complete but poststructuralists see them as fundamentally contradictory, open and unfinished **(49)**.

Ward says that Jacques Derrida's deconstructive work questions the meaning of meaning and sees words as having multiple meanings. "Deconstruction" is a process used to show the hidden assumptions of different fields of knowledge. One such assumption is that discourse about a particular field has a single subject, and that it is an object. Derrida deconstructs this by saying communication is a text and is subject to "differance" where the meaning of a word cannot be fixed and does not stand by itself but is part of a context of other words. Thus people interpret a word in different ways. No term has a fixed essence as it is defined in relation to what it is not, and is a differance. Texts strive to achieve a coherence but this is illusory and there is no fixed meaning to be found **(50)**.

Derrida also considered that we naturally think by way of opposites, such as public/private, body/soul, subject/object. There is no dialectical unity as one side is always preferred over the other and by analysing the relationship between the opposites then the power structure can be investigated. One term defines itself by way of rejecting the other term but it can often be found to have properties of the term that it rejects **(51)**.

Space is given for the arising of manifold interpretations and Derrida uses an idea, first proposed by Plato in the "Timaeus", of the Chora. Just as differance is a non-concept (unfixable) so the Chora is a non-space that is a condition and ground for things existing. It contains opposites in suspension and also in emergence so is not present or absent, is not being or non-being. Derrida describes the Chora as an empty space and a realm of possibility, in opposition to an actual revealing **(52)**.

According to Taylor, Derrida says, throughout his "Chora" essay, that "Plato figures chora as feminine – "the mother, the matrix, or the nurse." And yet, these "names" are improper, for chora is neither masculine not feminine but a third gender that approximates the neuter."" But if Derrida draws so closely on Plato then here is where his own position collapses, or is deconstructed, away from a third gender and into a bias towards the feminine **(53)**. This is the beginning of a move away from difference and towards a unity.

Ward describes how in "Revolution in Poetic Language" Julia Kristeva believes that a feminine perspective is preferable but that it is not timeless, essential or universal. Kristeva argues that women have been pushed to the boundaries in literature and art and that the non-essential voice from these boundaries is feminine. Masculine texts have features such as structure, intelligibility and stability so texts with diverse and unstable meanings can help to undermine male discourse. Male society rejects unfixed and multiple identities but varied use of language can increase the range of possible identities imaginable and free you from an imagined unity of the self. Progressive works of art for Kristeva are "fragmentary, incomplete, non-systematic and ultimately inexplicable." **(54)** This position remains divided but I will now argue that Georges Bataille takes it to an extreme that collapses into a transcendent unity.

A deconstructive, breakdown is further investigated by Taylor with the idea of Dionysian ritual. He explains how in "Theory of Religion" Bataille developed a rethinking of Friedrich Nietzsche's notions of the Apollonian and the Dionysian, argued for in "The Birth of Tragedy"**(55)**. Apollo is the ancient Greek god of the sun, music, poetry, morality, self-control and freedom from self control.

Dionysus is the ancient Greek god of wine, mystical ecstasy and intoxication. Neither can exist without the other. In Apollo we can achieve redemption within illusion but in Dionysus lays the return to the maternal womb of being. There is a lost intimacy found in the Dionysian realm that people long to return to and where the individual self disappears **(56)**. This being is the primordial oneness of Derrida's Chora **(57)** and it is here that I believe extreme division becomes a utopian unity.

The personality is disintegrated in a Dionysian style ritual. Difference is transformed into identity, and transgressive acts, that violate the boundaries between violence and eroticism, break down separation. Festivals are the place where this energy is most manifest. Sacrifice breaks the profane order and the greatest sacrifice is the self and selfhood, completed with death **(58)**.

This breakdown is a form of Gnostic Drama. Jane Goodall argues how the modernist theatre maker, Anton Artaud, believed that this original, cosmic presence was stolen and cannot be regained (prior to language). Artaud creates radical difference in his theatre in order to show the rationality that needs transcending. In Artaud's Gnostic drama cruelty meets cruelty in a sublime horror that is not just against language but against the body and the created world itself **(59)**. Artaud is fighting against the notion of a creator God/demiurge **(60)**

> "Artaud equates creation with cruelty and proposes to undertake the work of counter-cruelty in his theatre" **(61)**.

Artaud proposes a form of self-(re)creation where the human returns to Sophia, the "mother" of the demiurge. This is like the intuition of Schelling (as a way to fill the space created by the sublime dread invoked by Kant).

Taylor argues that modernism is associated with unity and utopia but that Postmodernism is associated with radical division. I argue that this radical division concludes in a spiritual gnosticism that, like Schelling's philosophy, is part of a philosophically modernist, spiritual enterprise. In contrast postmodern alternatives are non-extreme, non-radical positions. They allow people to live indecisively with the Kantian split between self and the world, with or without semi-ironic faith in a resolution in utopian unity.

The work of Bailey and Hirst glorifies in bloodletting and eroticism but also in the superficial world of fashion. They have commodified even the most severe of Dionysian imagery in order to provide a quick thrill. Nothing beyond is intimated or appealed to, there is no redemption for them. This work combines superficial fashion with deep religious issues but looks like a magazine shoot without any content or belief behind it. It does not take the Dionysian to its most fearful conclusion, it is less extreme and does not attempt to reach a conclusion beyond the importance of the artists.

Postmodern Religion

I am now going to argue that a position in opposition to this spiritual modernism and to Hirst's nihilism is Postmodern Religion. This is a combination of Derrida's views on Messianicity, the serious theology of Brian Walsh and the semi-irony of Victor E. Taylor. This position opens up the possibility of having diverse perspectives without collapsing into a complete deconstruction.

Derrida sees messianicity as not necessarily religious but as a rupture in horizons of expectation.

> "First name: the messianic, or messianicity without messianism. This would be the opening to the future or to the coming of the other as the advent of justice, but without horizon of expectation and without prophetic prefiguration." **(62)**

Messianism is an origin that is spontaneous and allows uprooting from dogmatism as it is open to, and expectant of, new perspectives linked to a faith in universal justice. However, it never allows those perspectives to be realised for as soon as one appears it is expectant of the next. **(63)**

Brian Walsh (Christian Reformed Chaplain to the University of Toronto) suggests that "what deconstruction requires is a non-determinate messianicity, a weak messianism that will not claim too much for itself." Walsh is convinced that this does not go far enough as the concept of Messianicity needs a determinate Messiah (perspective) for it to be fulfilled. He argues that Derrida rejects this because he is afraid of the judgement and warfare (or fascism) it could bring. **(64)**

I suggest that this tension between deconstruction and a constructive meaning could be resolved in a provisional and indefinite idea of a Messiah that allows space for "divine intervention" – but does not assume that it will occur.

An example of postmodern belief is given by Victor E. Taylor. He describes graveyard symbols that are almost completely areligious, where images of cars carved onto granite tombstones are shown as an expression of a person's hopes in the context of death that "unlike the Holy Cross, the Virgin Mary, an angel or other religious images," links to an ultimate that is "without resolution and without promise." **(65)**

The images offer no redemption or solace, only a semi-ironic belief, but are more pious and genuine as the makers recognise the failure of the overtly religious and provide their own provisional suggestion in face of the inadequacy of such representations. This expression still has passion and purpose and gives room for making a religious wish or prayer. There is no attempt to find an aesthetic, transcendent or political unity (like Schelling or Hegel's) just a semi-ironic faith not in science but in a higher power that can overcome problems that the believer is experiencing.

Irony uses meanings that are insincere and is related to parody or comic imitation. Michael Newman suggests that parody questions authority but that postmodernism has already removed authority. As a result Newman thinks that modernist parody questioned repressive authority but that postmodern parody just makes a nihilistic statement of resignation (as there is no absolute authority to parody) **(66)**. Thus I suggest that semi-parodic and semi-ironic expressions of religious faith involve a tension between nihilistic resignation and the questioning of belief structures. This tension and questioning remains hopeful that a "messianic" resolution can arise.

To clarify the concept of postmodern faith I will look at three classifications of religious faith given by Terrence W. Tilley in Postmodern theologies: the challenge of religious diversity. **(67)**

According to Tilley the term "Dissolution Postmodernism" sees the differences between religions with no absolute truth common to them apart from being without foundation (this is a feature of Hirst's work as he presents Christianity in a mocking way and is a feature of Borean's work as he presents all religions as commodities). A less extreme form this deconstruction is an ironic nihilism but an extreme form leads to a form of spiritual modernism. Neither of which fully qualifies as Postmodern religion.

According to Tilley the term "Constructive Postmodernism" sees the differences between religions as irreducible but that dialogue and public discourse can result in partial consensus where the "other" can remain "other" (this is a feature of Gupta's work as she gives various religious options within a framework of shared beliefs about worship).

A further position is "Theologies of Communal Practice" where, for Tilley, the believer can have faith in many different forms to suit different circumstances and relationships. This is like a constructive postmodernism but a uniting factor is the process of seeking truth rather than any actual truth claims (this is a feature of Gomez Pena's adaptation of different visual and musical forms in different artistic expressions and is also encouraged in Gupta's artistic use of the internet as a medium of religious expression).

Postmodern Religious Art

We can see how Hirst, Gomez Pena, Borean and Gupta fit into Tilley's groups. Dissolution postmodernism is deconstructive and Nihilistic whilst constructive postmodernism and theologies of communal practice share elements of partial, semi-ironic doctrinal belief or of artistic processes of believing. Next I look at how the artists' work relate to these postmodern religious positions.

Work with semi-ironic faith, eg Gupta's, contrasts with fully ironic, nihilistic works, eg Hirst's. Hirst's atheistic consumerism contradicts the religious theme of his work. This work contains a contrast of possibilities but the final authority of his nihilistic perspective is never in doubt. Such full irony and atheism is more modernist than the semi-irony of postmodernism.

Julian Stallabras describes Hirst's nihilistic work as being an unredemptive personal complicity with the market. This fits with the view that his work is an ironic comment, rather than being a religious statement. Hirst acts like a high priest of art commodity who sacrifices cows to aid in the creation of economic growth (a good harvest). An investment in his work is a status symbol and will potentially reap economic rewards (appreciation in value). His sacrificial cult is given a contemporary status but this dissolution postmodernism enslaves artist and buyer within an economic system, rather than liberate them from it, offer any positive direction or look at the tension between belief and unbelief.

Julian Stallabras sees the Young British Artists, like Hirst, as rejecting the deep psychology and metaphysics of traditional modern art **(68)** and as seeing social responsibility and moral sense as no longer ideologically possible **(69)**.

In their place the YBAs confront the viewer with the abject and destabilize fixed meaning. The work never makes closure and is not further justified or explained because the work has an anti-theoretical base and is autonomous from theory. Stallabras notes that the demise of the Avant-garde left no single, clear political stance and that the ideals of post modern orthodoxy have fallen to consumerism. **(70)**

In contrast Gomez Pena thinks that in postmodernity, religion is inevitably intertwined with pop and mass culture but that powerful political and religious symbols can be completely changed when put into new contexts. Such work inevitably implies political consequences because of the adverse reactions that it might generate and in Mexico this led to his work being trashed by religious fundamentalists outraged at his use of the Virgin Mary in 1983. **(71)**

Gomez Pena's political strategy is to constantly question and reinvent his identity **(72)**. This challenges authority but in his performance lecture the atmosphere was of an exotic, entertaining carnival, freak-show or museum, where guns and sex mix together with cultural artefacts. These different combinations gave no real progression and felt very superficial even though they were to make an important statement. There didn't seem to be a strong connection between the theatrical action and the deeper message.

In the performance, physical, bodily suffering connected to a deeper message of political and bodily resurrection. This was a powerful metaphor on a religious level, relating to sacrifice and ritual, but there was no stated intention that the performance might work as a genuine religious rite and it did not make a space for semi-ironic worship. The performance lecture created a space for a political assertion to be made. This is a political/artistic modernist strategy, to influence mass thinking by critical, political art. To be effective, Gomez Pena needs to have the media visibility of Hirst and Bailey to provide a popular view that will change patterns of consumption and inspire in a direction of equality and community.

Gomez Pena seeks to achieve political change but, despite his use of toy weapons, he is still within a modernist, non-religious, political model that is oppositional to commodity and has no irony. I think that unless Gomez Pena's practice is semi-ironic then it is more modernist and about political results than postmodern. Viewed in isolation from its political content, however, his eclectic work is an ongoing, postmodern, communal practice (of artistic opposition to commodity culture) that is neither constructive nor dissolution postmodernism.

In contrast a statement of a complete relation to consumerism is made in Borean's website:

> "This is the concept behind the Plug 'n' Pray concept: religion is no longer a spiritual   experience or a personal journey to get closer to our transcendent inner dimension – it belongs now to the FCG (Fast Consumer Goods) segment." **(73)**

Religious consumerism is the direct subject matter of Plug 'n' Pray whereas Hirst's subject is religion put into a consumable, and marketed, high-art/fashion format. Both artworks are fully ironic so are not fully postmodern and offer no real opportunity of transformation, political or personal. Consumerism of religious goods is not enough as there needs to be something more than purchasing for the work to be termed religious.

In considering the term Postmodern Religious Art, we have rejected deeper spirituality as being modernist and as not having a postmodern concern with the latest superficialities. Postmodern religions should be translated into commodities, like "Plug 'n' Pray", yet maintain transformative possibilities. Such a semi-ironic religious commodity would give space for a non simulated, non-commodifiable change/effect in peoples' lives. The basis of constructive postmodern religious art is a superficial religious commodity which semi-ironically allows the possibility of the occurrence of utopian religious changes.

Heidi Reitmaier, External Events Officer at the Tate Modern, notes how Gupta suggests that the "real" nature of the blessing received is dependent on the belief of the user. Reitmaier says that Gupta's work is nuanced. It proposes a series of spiritual options without definite solutions. It is non-prescriptive and facilitates questioning. Reitmaier also suggests that there is "a sense of flippancy and disregard were it not for the more profound questions raised about the present status of ancient faiths." **(74).**

You question your motives and the relevance, or importance, of this work as you move through the stages of the blessing. Reitmaier says that the site invites a "subjective, highly personal, incoherent and accumulative" interaction but also asks the user to reflect on their own interests in the issues of " the complications of global religions" **(75).**

Although Gupta's postmodern religious art has the form of commodity, irony and the secular, a semi-ironic space is made for a break through to non-commodifiable, sincere and sacred sentiments. This may bring about utopian change but such change is constructive postmodernism as it arises out of a semi-ironic religious faith, rather than modernist dialectics, spiritualism or scientific progress.

In "What Happened to Religion in Contemporary Art?" James Elkins writes how Slavoj Zizek described God as the ultimate *tamagochi* (a Japanese hand held game where you feed and entertain an imaginary pet). In this toy our compassion has been channelled into a private computer game about a God that puts demands upon us **(76)**. Gupta has taken this further in the work "God.exe" **(77)**. "God.exe" gets to the crux of the issue. Is it real prayer or just a simulation of prayer that we make to the tamagochi. I was led to question my relationship to the idea of God and was open to trying prayer in an internet context. A spirit of open enquiry was required as an experiment both in belief in god, and methods of prayer. Perhaps the only answer to these questions can come if there is an answer to the prayers that you make.

A weakened form of Utopian thinking can give either the non-transcendent Nihilism of Hirst (dissolution postmodernism) or a semi-ironic faith of Gupta (constructive postmodernism). Both of these can have a constantly developing theology of communal practise (as of Gomez Pena).

Taylor argued that both the transcendent art, of modernism, and the immanent pop art, of "modernist postmodernism", were concerned with utopia. His view was that modernism is characterised by utopian thinking and that radical division characterises postmodern thinking. I argued that the radical division is characterised by spiritual gnosticism and that postmodern religion does not assert single solutions and is semi-ironic, about radical division, nihilism and utopian unity.

Rather than spirituality, aesthetics, politics or technology being the focus of art I propose that religion is reappearing in art but this time in the semi-ironic form of Postmodern Religious Art. Kant's aesthetic and spiritual dread and helplessness at the sublime in nature is semi-overcome with a semi-ironic faith in the power of a religious commodity. Whether this semi-ironic faith can lead to any personal, physical or critical/political change is not part of the scope of this thesis.

Conclusion

Finally we can evaluate the relationship between choice of medium and the religious and political effectiveness of the work of Hirst, Gomez Pena, Borean and Gupta.

An installation such as Hirst's creates a religious environment that mimics a church but remains clearly a gallery. This is appropriate to how his photographs are also seen as mimicking, rather than becoming, religious art. Gomez Pena creates a makeshift sacred space and then performs an actual ritual in that space, activating that environment and creating a closer parallel to religion. However, the work does not engage with genuine religious faith in order to take on an extra, supernatural element (essential to religion). Gomez Pena also rejects the consumer polish of a gallery and does not engage so closely with the tensions between postmodernism and consumerism as Plug 'n' Pray and Hirst. Plug 'n' Pray has a religious subject matter but there is no reality to it as it is completely virtual and offers nothing religious other than imagery.

Only Gupta engages with consumerism, genuine religious content and with performance (through attending rituals, using appropriate imagery and inviting the audience to take part in the rituals). Her work, however, differs to Hirst's and Gomez Pena's as nothing physical is created (other than a downloadable certificate). Her artwork is a tool for creating a religious expression, rather than being the religious expression itself. Her medium, the internet, has modernist, technological and spiritual associations and her website is a structure Gupta could also use it for oppression.

The artists above engage with issues of Postmodern Religious Art and this thesis has articulated what some of these issues are. None of their works fit exactly the definition but Gupta's work most clearly shows this position is not just theoretical and is being developed in art practice in a number of ways.

31 October 2004

Essay 8.

POSTMODERN RELIGIOUS ART –
FROM LIMINALITY TO MESSIANICITY

Brian Walsh (Christian Reformed Chaplain to the University of Toronto) claims in his web article *"Derrida and the Messiah: The Spiritual Face of Postmodernity"*, that because Modernism linked to humanism, so postmodernism might re-link to the religious. **(1)**

Woodhead and Heelas say that there is a widespread suspicion of grand narratives in postmodern thinking but dominance of the secularisation theory (that religion was in decline) was unquestioned in much of the twentieth century. Now a sacralization model has arisen due to evidence of religious vitality in much of the world. **(2).**

In this article I combine parts of my MA thesis "Is it possible to have Postmodern Religious Art and Performance?" (Wimbledon School of Art, London, 2003) with my own small narrative, and a few of the revelations and prophecies I experienced, as a way to look at a definition of postmodern religious art.

In the late 80s and early 1990s I trained as a philosopher and I was an agnostic fascinated with religion.

Many of my friends were Evangelical Christians who emphasised expressive worship, the power of prayer to bring material change and manifestations of the Spirit. I couldn't accept such blind faith but became open to revelation by being in Quaker meetings, where the Spirit can speak, through people.

I was like the figure in Kaspar David Friedrich's "Wanderer above the Sea of Fog", c.1818. Joseph Leo Koerner, Assistant Professor of Fine Art at Harvard University, argues that this Romantic figure serves as an indication of our relation to the landscape and the infinite, but at one remove. For Koerner, the forms that arise out of the fog relate to a state of creative and spiritual possibilities **(3)**. Koerner thinks that the viewer approaches a pantheistic dissolution into the infinite background of nature by way of that figure **(4)**.

I was in London restoring historic churches, teaching religious education, carving figurative sculpture and doing interfaith work when I entered Friedrich's Fog and I had a mystical experience of non-duality – beyond conceptual oppositions such as being and nothingness. This mystical experience was of a transcendence of moral struggle but goodness and moral revelation were the values that I believed in so I could not accept the mystics' path.

David K Clark & Norman L. Geisler, two Christian theologians, argue against mysticism.

"Pantheists who use a mystical way of knowing must try somehow to distinguish two modes of knowing, the mystical mode and the empirical mode. The first of these is unitive, unmediated, nonconceptual, nonlogical and noninferential. By contrast, the second is divided, conceptual, logical, and inferential." **(5)**

"The move to discredit ordinary modes of knowing in favor of the higher mystical mode of knowing depends on the logical distinction between the two modes of knowing. Far from overcoming rational principles, this move affirms them." **(6)**

Thus, the philosophical problem with non-dualism is that there is a dualism between it and dualism. Thus dualism is more real but I still needed to integrate with my mystical experience.

I felt a call to pilgrimage and I received a sign at Westminster Quaker Meeting House, London in 1994. When I questioned whether we need religious buildings there was thunder and lightning directly over the meeting house. I came out of the meeting and saw a book on the table about the reconstruction of Jerusalem, by the modern architect Moshe Safdie.

I felt that Jerusalem was the center of religious conflict and where I could find if religious art has value. There I worked on ancient sites with the Israeli, British and Palestinian Archaeological Authorities (1995-6).

I was profoundly affected by the physical beauty of the land, history and rituals of Jews, Christians, Muslims and Bahais – but I felt that something was missing. There was a split between sacred and secular society and conflicts between faith groups due to their literal interpretations of their own scripture but a loose interpretations of the scriptures of others.

At this point I was exploring notions of the relation of dualism to non-dualism, of Messiahship and of forgiveness in each of these traditions. Forgiveness was essential to me as a concept that broke through karmic law and produced a dualistic goodness over a non-dualistic balancing.

Whilst I was in the Holy Land I felt compelled to pray and made a series of abstract expressionist paintings at the Dome of the Rock, Jerusalem and at the Bahai Gardens, Acco. This was a media I would not usually work in and related to non-duality.

This painting followed in the tradition of Modern artists who sought to reconcile the Romantics' contrasts of the figure and the landscape through mystical abstraction.

John Golding, painter, curator and art historian, argues that Mondrian followed Hegel's dialectic and his view that art, without an explicit religious content, was a way towards God. Golding says that Mondrian was influenced by Madame Blavatsky's Theosophical view that evolution occurs through the balancing of opposites. Mondrian believed in a continually changing process (influenced by Blavatsky's view that fluidity and water are the fundamental reality) (7) so his work displays a visual rhythm, throb and dynamism.

Golding also thinks that flat, abstract art is more truthful than illusionism on a painted surface so Mondrian's surface becomes the whole image – and not just representations within a surface (8). Eg "Composition with Yellow, Red, Black, Blue and Grey ", oil on canvas, 1920 and used flatness in order to bring the spiritual near to the viewer **(9)**.

Golding later says that Jackson Pollock's abstraction was influenced by Jungian psychology, by Jung's symbolic systems, by the idea of the individual delving into their own unconscious **(10)** and by the Surrealist's notion of automatic drawing.

By pure energy/action and the gesture itself was seen as a hermetic symbol, eg "Full Fathom Five", oil on canvas, 1947. The work was made of short, rhythmic strokes that cancel each other in the overall surge of the painting **(11)**. He tried to link man and the eternal in his art **(12)** by directly confronting the person standing before the work with the forces of nature **(13)**.

Mark Rothko continued this confrontation and engulfed his viewers in his dark, profound colour paintings eg "No.10", 1950, Oil on canvas, 1950.   These acted like doorways through the infinite, passing through a dividing line that is like the horizon point of Friedrich's landscape. Rothko was influenced by the Qabbalah (Jewish mysticism) as was Barnett Newman where "Onement I", oil on canvas 1948_relates to the twelfth century Qabbalistic text the Zohar, which describes the unity of male and female principles, from which the divine light emanated.

This mysticism is part of a modernist perspective but I think that the work of these artists is problematic as their grand syntheses were mainly abstract and not a synthesis with figurative art. Clement Greenberg argued, in his influential 1939 essay Avant-Garde and Kitsch, that the avant-garde was concerned with innovation and progress but fascist countries used kitsch in order to keep them connected with the masses and as a way to revere past-masters and historical culture. True socialism would give the right conditions for education so that people can appreciate true (ie. avant-garde and abstract) culture **(14)**.

I think that with the Nazi Holocaust there came a crisis in faith in God and in Grand Narratives of progress. Religious and Fascist kitsch and narrative was rejected in favour of abstraction.

Figurative art could be seen all around Jerusalem in the form of Christian kitsch and I found the style, and the way effigies were used in ritual, to be religiously inspiring. Andy Warhol rejected modernism and used religious kitsch as an updated expression, one of empty consumerism. Warhol is associated with atheism but Warhol used mass produced Catholic images in works like "The Last Supper" series 1986.

In his survey, of the American avant-garde since 1970, Henry. M. Sayre, Associate Professor of art at Oregon University states how Andy Warhol's "Maos" 1974 and "Hammer and Sickles" 1976 gave an empty reminder of how the political nature of art could be turned into commodity (even as "Mao Wallpaper"). Warhol thought that the only way to critique this commodity system is in the commodity marketplace (as even the avant-garde had become a marketable notion). The current avant-garde must accept their market status to attempt to overcome it **(15)** but, in his paper for the 1985 ICA conference on Postmodernism, Michael Newman questions how far Warhol was complicit in pop culture and how far he was deconstructing it. Even deconstruction can be seen as careerist opportunism on the part of the artist **(16)**.

In his article "Warhol's Madonna", Guiseppe Frangi says that Warhol was a regular attending Greek Catholic **(17)** so I suggest that Warhol attempted to express issues of salvation through commodity in what Professor Dr Jane Daggett Dilenberger (of the Graduate Theological Union of Berkeley) describes as the largest body of religious works by any major contemporary American artist **(18)**.

I think that the Catholic eucharist is an immanent theology, where Christians believe, that by consuming the Eucharist they are restored in the moral world and this consumer tension is approached in Warhol's work.

Back in the UK I worked on my own pop art, a 30 centimetre millennium sculpture of a Babylonian angel scanned into computer, scaled and manufactured at 2 metres. This was made using the latest aerospace computer manufacturing technology.

I was also resident with Loughborough University's Creativity and Cognition Research Unit exploring interactive computer sensor environments. The programmes that I ran came out with the unexpected consequence of creating mandalas and swastikas. These mystical symbols were unintended and I began to have mild telepathic experiences afterwards.

It was at this point that I began to see the contrast between mysticism, represented in interactive performance in abstract environments and moralism, represented in narrative sculpture. I thought that by linking them together that art can make a link between mystical and moral consciousness that could not be made philosophically. I outlined a relation between this idea and the history of world religious art and called my work The Ism, a play on the word theism.

I wrote about this perspective in my article "Digital Spirituality" (19) and I launched The Ism on Millennium Eve at the Golden Gate, Jerusalem, where the Messiah or Jesus is supposed to arrive for Jews, Christians and Muslims. I wanted to create an abstract expressionist art work that captured any spiritual change at the turn of the millennium. This performance was webcast by MessiahCAM, but was stopped by Israeli police. This confiscation integrated the police into the performance – emphasizing forgiveness and inclusivity. Next day I sent information on The Ism to 300 art critics first post of the new millennium from Jerusalem.

This was "prophetic" as in 2001 a peace activist group formed to address the Palestinian problem. This group is called the International Solidarity Movement, or the ISM for short. (20)

I continued with my abstract expressionist experiments and in 2000 created the rainbow swastika symbol. Use of this symbol questions whether the Messiah's forgiveness could even extend to the Holocaust. The swastika is associated with Nazism only in the first world and I reclaim it as a symbol of peace. It is a Hindu symbol of good luck that relates to pure, mystical energy. I have combined it with the rainbow, a symbol of the new age, gay rights and god's reconciliation after the Biblical flood. After I started to use this symbol I then discovered that I am Jewish. I also discovered a

Jewish website, arguing against New Age philosophy and how it was linked to Nazism, called "The Rainbow Swastika" by Hannah Newman **(21)**

I then integrated this swastika into figurative work and images, following the dialectical structure of The Ism. I presented this structure in papers at conferences, illustrated with my Game of World Religious Art. **(22) (23)**

My work resembled liminality as described by Susan Broadhurst:

> "liminal performance similarly presents a deconstruction of binary opposition, which is demonstrated in the collapse of hierarchical distinctions such as those between high and mass/ popular culture." **(24)**

Liminality relates to a state of non-dualism, as it is a state between opposites – often seen as a creative, magical space where ideas can become actualised. So liminality is a suspension of closure and reason, where the artist preferences the non-dual and gives space for a mystic transcendence.

My work needed to move on from this as I believe that the artist's energy needs channelling into a positive moral effect and not just a mystical experience. In so far as The Ism resembles the liminal it is modernist, so I needed a postmodern expression.

These issues relate to Derrida's distinction between Messianicity and the Chora. Derrida sees Messianicity as not necessarily religious but as a rupture in expectation. It is linked to a rational realization that belief in rational systems is not founded on the laws contained in the system but on a faith that is spontaneous and quasi automatic. This Messianic faith, in allowing of uprooting from dogmatism, allows universal rationality and political democracy by looking expectantly to new faith perspectives.

Derrida describes the Chora as an empty space as used by Plato and Plotinus and continued by Heidegger. This Chora is seen as a realm of possibility, in opposition to the actual revealing of a religion. **(25)** The Chora is a liminal space.

This Chora gives open, aesthetic possiblity but I seek to channel possibility into a definite, historical, political form of Messianicity.

Warhol's form of postmodern religious art celebrated consumer kitsch and immanent salvation but did not hold a promise of personal or political change nor of divine intervention.

On the political effects of art Bonito Oliva, Professor of Institutions of Art History at the Faculty of Architecture of the University of Rome, proposed that art now operates like a game without political challenge **(26)**. He proposed that the historic avant-garde was involved in a dialectical progression of reuniting opposites but in contrast to this the Trans-avantgarde reject ideological progress, preferring to imitate and fragment various historical art forms **(27)** Instead of a grand avant-garde synthesis there is just an eclectic use of diverse imagery. Figurative elements are joined with abstract elements, and historical art images are linked with popular culture **(28)** but the appropriation is ironic, liminal, without cohesion, synthesis or political direction **(29)** and is just another marketable commodity.

I think that religious subjects in art can produce a politically explosive effects by creating a fear of terrorist reactions of the Other –and a fear of divine retribution for blasphemy. Thus postmodern mixing of religious styles, could lead to an economic renegotiation with the Other – to stop the Other from violently reacting.

On the divine effects of art I think that an attempt to explain how belief can arise out of postmodern liminality is given in Para/Inquiry: Postmodern Religion and Culture by Victor E. Taylor, who teaches in the Department of English and Humanities at York College of Pennsylvania and is editor of the Journal for Cultural and Religious Theory.

Taylor gives an example of the Parasacred as being graveyard symbols that are almost completely areligious. Images of cars carved on to granite tombstones are shown as an expression of a person's hopes in the context of death and of their gravest fears and doubts, but "unlike the Holy Cross, the Virgin Mary, an angel or other religious images," the car links to an ultimate that is "without resolution and without promise."

The images offer no redemption or solace, only parasacrality. "The car opens the "Ultimate" to a "plural ultimate" that is "para", "alongside, beside, and a subsidiary of the sacred." **(30)**

Taylor sees the representation of a footballer as more pious and genuine as it recognises the failure of the overtly religious and provides its own suggestion of the inadequacy of such representations.

I think that a postmodern religious expression is unable to be fully religious, but can still have passion and purpose. The expression gives room for a miracle to occur and many people need to express that possibility and to make individual wishes.

Simulation is an important notion for Newman and traces its origin to Jean Baudrillard. Baudrillard argues that our image of reality begins as a reflection of reality, then becomes a mask of reality, then marks an absence of reality and then bears no relation to reality at all, and is, in fact, a pure simulacrum **(31)**. Signs no longer have a meaning as nothing is true and false. Newman concludes that for Baudrillard simulation is not a belief in total difference but in the melancholy at the total sameness of everything that cannot be seen as original, nor as copy.

As a result, a postmodern religious art would take historical images of images of religion and mixes them in non dogmatic pictures of reality, that are provisional myths that allow for creative revelation.

The mixing of religious simulations is not a parody or blasphemy but rather as a para-sacrality, where the institutional religions are deconstructed but are then reconstructed as individual simulations.

These simulations might facilitate a revelation as although postmodern religious art has the form of commodity, irony and the secular, space is made for the parasacred to break through to non-commodifiable, sincere and sacred sentiments in the supernatural forms of revelation, coincidence, miracle and healing.

Walsh suggests that Derrida terms Messianicity as a human expectation of a Messiah that cannot be fulfilled in a determinate, undeconstructible way. "what deconstruction requires is a non-determinate messianicity, a weak messianism that will not claim too much for itself." Walsh is convinced that the concept of Messianicity needs a determinate Messiah to be fulfilled and that Derrida rejects this because he is afraid of the judgement and warfare it could bring.

I propose that the postmodern religion is not just a conflictual, deconstructive liminality, but a constructive entertainment of a parasacred diversity of mythic, anthropological, moral and Messianic meanings. I think we can have a provisional, non-specific and indefinite idea of a Messiah that allows space for provisional revelation and actual religious experience, free-will and miraculous non-causal change.

To clarify the concept of postmodern religion I will look at some classifications of religious faith given by Terrence W. Tilley in Postmodern theologies: the challenge of religious diversity. Pluralism is that we cannot know, for sure, which of a number of belief systems is correct. Particularism is that all religious traditions are substantially different and cannot make claims about traditions outside their own **(32)**.

Tilley thinks that pluralists minimize or erase the differences among religious traditions and particularists are irreducibly diverse and "do not deny the otherness of the "other"". Tilley concludes that pluralists fail to take difference and otherness between religions seriously, so are not postmodern religious thinkers (as they posit a modernist, core spirituality) **(33)**.

Dissolution Postmodernism sees an essential difference between religions with no absolute truth common to them apart from being without foundation.

Constructive Postmodernism sees differences between religions as irreducible but that dialogue and public discourse can result in partial consensus (where the "other" can remain "other").

A further position is Theologies of Communal Practice which accepts pluralism and diversity as being integral but the believer can have faith in many different forms to suit different circumstances and relationships. This is like a constructive postmodernism but the additional uniting factor is the process of seeking truth rather than any actual truth claims **(34)**.

Linda Woodhead and Paul Heelas, the editors of <u>Religion in Modern Times</u>, predict the future of postmodern religion. They feel that "de-essentialized postmodern religions that attempt to deconstruct the categories of self, God, and religion are unlikely to have a great influence outside the academy. Religions outside such circles are strongly essentialised; it is hard to see how they could perform social, political, salvific and moral tasks if they were not.**(35)**" Thus religions of particularism are predicted as the most popular in times of political unrest.

I think, however, that this overlooks that religion might be radically altered. Rather than maintained as oppositional to commerce, de-essentialized postmodern religions will be complicit with the market-place. This constructive postmodernism united by a theology of communal practice (linked to commerce, art and lifestyle options) would not be pluralist in belief, just a superficial addition over the basic market structure of modernism but capable of producing fundamentally "Other" effects (and not just a modernist mystical union). Such a postmodern religion would initially create political unrest and condemnation because of protest from non-commodified religious groups.

I think that Postmodern religion is a constructive Postmodernism where art and consumerism are important elements of a theology of communal practice. These postmodern beliefs are unverifiable hypotheses that are necessary for human life. Modern findings of science and politics are the core and the postmodern veneer is the lifestyles, products and viewpoints that can be chosen.

There is concern from Lawrence. R Moore, in his study of American religion in the marketplace, that as a subject of the market, religion is being trivialised and losing its transformative power and that providing of charitable works cannot be reduced solely to commodity status. I think, however, that Religion can be commodified in the parasacred but where the non simulated, non-commodifiable aspect can break through into peoples lives.

Moore thinks that the US separation of church from state, meant that religion already competes in the marketplace with other goods and services and that a benefit of this is that the market also provides a framework for religious debate and relations that was less tolerant in earlier cultures **(36)**.

Woodhead and Heelas say that Rodney Start arguing in <u>Bringing Theory Back In</u>, **(37)** describe other benefits of religious consumerism. With a pluralist religious economy, religions specialise and cater for special needs and tastes of specific market segments. This leads to a higher degree of participation as religions meet the needs of a greater number of consumers.

To be a responsible consumer I think that education is required but principles of the separation of church and state were written into the United States constitution so there is no state religious education and beliefs are supposed to be kept separate from the government. This has meant that the religious education of US citizens has become provincial.

Religious belief has often been seen as compensation for poverty and poor countries are often fundamentalist. So why is the US is both rich and strongly religious. US poverty is possibly from its lack of social cohesion. By keeping religion and state separate there is no common identity other than patriotism. I suggest that this cohesion should be provided through an educational process, a theology of communal practice of creative consumerism.

In contrast Great Britain linked religion with state and education and the nature of religious education changed to reflect the immigration of diverse faith groups. As a result the UK government is far more open to varied religious viewpoints and has recently moved to include representatives from diverse faith groups in governmental decision-making **(38)**.

Can such a Postmodern process of religious liberalisation counter religious violence? Benjamin R. Barber is the Whitman Professor of Political Science at Rutgers University and Director of the Walt Whitman Center for the Culture and Politics of Democracy. In <u>Jihad vs McWorld : Terrorism's Challenge to Democracy</u>, he proposes that the modern world and global culture is being torn apart by two forces, those of corporate, economic primacy and those of national/religious fundamentalism. He thinks that both forces are inherently totalitarian and inimical to democracy which must be based on active civic participation. **(39)**

Barber suggests that the free market is non-democratic but I suggest that it is just that the control of the market is by monopolies that do not allow the postmodern nature of the market to appear. Modernism gives the trade structure and McWorld and Jihad should be just two commodities/lifestyle options to choose.

I think they can both operate as consumer/lifestyle options that do not undermine the modernist basic economic conditions for free-market choice (including religious choice).

I suggest that religious democracy will only follow if economic equality is created. Without this equality a basic religious sentiment is offended and this sentiment is prior to economic and political concerns. Countries subjected to social injustice by the first world reject political modernism as a viable alternative and adopt fundamental forms of religion.

Patrice Pavis, the editor of <u>The Intercultural Performance Reader</u>, worries that interculturalism is just an appropriation of other cultures by a dominant culture that will destroy the cultures which it assimilates **(40)**. The appearance of a global culture is not democratic but is really the subsuming of all individual cultures under the dominant West (consumerism) **(41)**.

In The Intercultural Performance Reader Rustom Bharucha suggests that materials, methods and processes are inseparably linked to the narratives and performances of other cultures. He thinks that there is appropriation of foods, music, clothing and ritual styles but ignorance about the political crisis (eg famine and war) that those countries are involved in **(42)**. Thus, they take without offering any aid.

Clive Barker who, also in The Intercultural Performance Reader, believes that intercultural relations should be grounded in practical activities that must arise out of cultures of conflict and not be appropriated images imposed on those cultures from outside. The work must arise from the communities where the conflicts arise. **(43)**.

I think that these points do not account for the fact that postmodernism is a democratisation and not a colonialzation. Postmodern religious art is a heresy to non-democratic religious monopolies and may be considered blasphemous, but I feel that a multicultural society should allow articulation of blasphemy. Many religious texts are blasphemy to other religions and compromise is necessary if people are to be brought together for market equality.

A structure that involves the different religious community groups in a democratic consultative process should be created, based on education, choice and economic opportunities.

The links that I want to make require years of building of relations, but I feel that by focussing on the irreconcilable details of religions that division is created. In contrast art can break down theological barriers to advertise a way to bring people together.

Relations might be built by giving economic aid to people and countries and providing successful media campaigns to promote this religious democratisation.

Barber suggests that statistically the information and entertainments sector is the most financially powerful and controls the manufacturing and agricultural industries. Barber shows the media sector is capable of bringing change about through advertising and media images **(44).**

I think that art can be effective when it serves as advertising or promotional materials for lifestyle and behaviour changes in relation to tourism, fashion, music, religious and consumer products.

Bharucha also notes that religious difference as a cause of violence is reported by the media but none of the initiatives of reconstruction are represented. Democratic protests are ignored in the actions of governments and this perpetuates the cultures of difference **(45).** I question whether art be taken up by the media unless it had explosive consequences, had many artists working in this way or had the art world heavily funding such work.

An alternative may be the production of iconic works that will create a postmodern religious climate. This will give people options on how to combine, liberalise and change traditional views. Such work inevitably implies political consequences because of the adverse reactions that it might generate from fundamentalists.

Although the artist may have had personal revelations, they encourage people to have their own revelations. It is not an attempt to found a new religion (pre-modern) but to create conditions whereby other people feel free to create their own religions, narratives, icons (commodities) and rituals.

Postmodern religious art is not about the specifics of the religions nor about a general mysticism or doctrine. It is concerned with the common practice of experimental methods and beliefs for ritual, artistic, musical, fashion and architectural activities.

In the UK club nights like "Escape from Samsara","Kundalini", "Tribalism" and "Planet Angel" tend to be influenced by Paganism and Eastern, non-dualistic religions. The emphasis in these clubs is on Ecstasy, dancing, loud techno, tribal rhythms, interactive games and psychedelic environments

In contrast, Gay Disco clubs have a dualistic religious dimension, such as "Heaven", "Salvation" and "Sanctuary". These clubs often pay limited reference to religious traditions they are named after and focus on the kitsch visuals of the tradition, rejecting any deeper meaning. There is an interest in physical appearances alcohol, dancing and sexual encounter in these clubs. The gay scene is often symbolized with a rainbow flag but the rainbow is also a symbol used in the New Age clubbing.

I wanted to link religious consumerism, ritual and artwork in Disco Art Religion. This is a celebratory reconciliation of cultural and religious opponents in a common, consumer humanity. Here I incorporate popular cultural forms of kitsch, clubbing, music, fashion, sculpture, disco lights, mirror balls and neon signs.

My "scene" included Club Religion, an "Interreligious Fancy Dress and Fashion Launch Party" at the Arts Café and Golders Green Unitarian Church 2002, accompanied with a series of mock fashion adverts for religion in a consumer world.

My rituals involved sacrificing a cake that the audience has iced whilst dressed in rainbow coloured robes and under disco lighting. This Holy communion was linked to children's birthday parties to shows the universal energies involved in ritual and channelled in individual wishing.

On Hannukah (December 7[th)] 2002, dressed as an interreligious prophet of Disco Art Religion (wearing items from Judaism, Christianity, Islam, Hinduism, Buddhism and New York Disco) I created Eve II, the Disco Art Messiah, at Ground Zero. She was painted with a rainbow swastika then dressed in Israeli flag (Star of David) nappies and given a disco bopper halo.

Coincidentally, on December 27th 2002 the Raelian society (which believes world religions were the revelation of aliens) announced the birth of a cloned a human baby, Eve. The coincidence was even more striking, when I discovered that the original symbol of the Raelians was a swastika within a Star of David. **(46)**

Eve II symbolically returned a Big Apple (New York) to the tree of knowledge of good and evil (a tree at Ground Zero) and went on to find the tree of life (the Rockerfeller Christmas Tree) to symbolise giving world economic aid.

After going on an interreligious picnic in the Garden of Eden (Long Meg Neolithic Stone circle in the Eden Valley , UK) on new year's day 2003, Eve II next appeared at my exhibition "Stop Armageddon" (coinciding with the Anti War demonstrations) near Trafalgar Square, London, in the Westminster Quaker Gallery, March 2003. Manikins sat in the lounge "watching" my DVD of the birth of EVE II with nursery, and playroom behind.

Eve II was in an interreligious golden disco crib. Behind her was "GOD?" in neon and the golden void re-birthday balloon (symbolizing the Chora that creation comes out of). This presented religious ritual options, open to both believer and non-believer. GOD? Has a question mark because there is a decision to suspend judgement for the purpose of coming together in moral community – thus placing morals above GOD and religion but allowing GOD to break through via the Parasacred.

"GOD?" in neon oversees Eve II's crib situated between two Christmas trees one with fairy lights (the tree of life) and one with plastic apple and inflatable serpent (tree of knowledge).

In the opening of "Stop Armageddon", EVE II, was symbolically used to sacrifice a plastic red heffer (needed to restore temple sacrifice) for world peace. This heffer was then installed like a miniature Damien Hirst sculpture in the temple.

This put an abomination in the temple – that the antichrist is supposed to do. The antichrist is associated with the devil and tempter in the garden of Eden and in Jewish Qabbalah the number of the tempter (Nashad) is the number of the Messiah. By throwing away moral exclusivity this emphasized equality and forgiveness.

The Temple was one building of many in the "New Jerusalem". Kitsch buildings, statues from many religions and Jesus with Krishna racing on scalextric were combined in Eve II's playroom.

Kitsch presents a gulf between what is and an ideal world – and it presents a mass production and a common sentiment, often of a superficial, rather than a deep inner, spirituality.

Few people are interested in modernism's workings, rather they are just interested in the positive, postmodern consumer lifestyle effects that modernism brings. Modernism is the necessary base out of which the superficial arises. The relationship between the two can be expressed in works of art but the abstract mechanics are secondary to the hope that kitsch art creates.

I had begun my journey from the Quaker meeting house, to explore the relation of art and religion in Jerusalem and had returned with a vision of a "New Jerusalem" where the religious forms are valued and important but should not interfere with modernism's call for basic human rights.

We need a revelation to convince us of the effectiveness of both religion and forgiveness to provide us with the strength to implement it in our lives. We need faith to go the extra mile, without compromising on following basic modernist assumptions of human rights etc.

Within seconds of closing the door on my exhibition the bulb of the main disco light behind "GOD?" blew out. Was this a sign from GOD??

The exhibition was ignored by media so did not generate controversy or debate. Hopefully my recent painting "The Eve II Revelation", acrylic on canvas, 100 x 127cm, 2003, will get more interest. This follows in the tradition of Kaspar David Friedrich but the figures have turned round. An image can also be seen on (47)

Eve II, a parasacred messiah, breaks throught the abstractions of Modernism to give a revelation to a group of myself dressed in assorted costumes of prophets. It symbolises how we choose from a range of religious options but have to wait for revelation.

The figure breaks out of liminality and expresses Messianicity. It nods to modernist non-duality for its origin but calls for moral action by questioning cultural and religious dogmatism. I use technical skill to channel sublime and mystical energy into a moral form.

I posed for the painting photograph on top of a Great Gable in the Lake District (birth place of English Romaniticism). On the final pose, where I was naked, out of the clouds, in exactly the place where Eve II would appear, a rescue helicopter appeared. This was both a shock and a validating revelation as I quickly rushed to grab my clothes.

Postmodern religious art seeks to make a space for faith and for moral goodness to be created that is over and above non-dualistic Karmic balancing. The result of failing to get media interest I my work I am attempting to make Morecambe, a seaside town in the north of England, into a world centre for Postmodern religious art.

This project looks at how pilgrimage and visiting a seaside resort have a number of things in common. It highlights that the traditional, white catchment of visitors has been replaced by many Hindu, Muslim and Sikh communities but the marketing of this resort remains directed at a white audience.

I have advertised for people to make seaside pilgrimage and build their own religion, in my interreligious flat on Morecambe promenade, exhibiting kitsch momentos, interreligious rituals and Morecambe's sublime scenery. The opening celebrations were on 30TH December 2003 and included a 5-tier interreligious wedding cake, gambling machine, 7 inflatable disciples, a swing/belly hybrid dancer, a gingerbread person pilgrimage to models of religious buildings and the interreligious disco line dance.

The interreligious wedding cake has been used performancein the "Lets Get Married" art wedding day at Grizedale Arts, Cumbria, and shown at St Saviours church, behind Harrods, London. It represents famous Christian, Muslim, Jewish, Buddhist and Daoist buildings. It was an idea that I had and then could actualise when I coincidentally met a cake designer, Stephanie T Sturges, who became my girlfriend.

The flat is open throughout 2004 by appointment and will be part of a local diversity festival. Eve II is currently residing in the Morecambe flat.

20 July 2004

Essay 9.

A DEFINITION OF POSTMODERN RELIGIOUS ART

This perspective is a rejection of the central perspectives of Modernism. It is not to be confused with a focus on mysticism or spirituality that arose in Modern art thought. It is a view that part held by many people without realising they hold it.

It is a return to fideism but with characteristics of postmodernism and not with characteristics of pre-modern religion.

These characteristics include bricolage, superficiality, consumerism, semi-irony, lack of a single meaning.

Important to the debate on whether postmodernism is just part of Late Capitalism is the belief that "postmodern religious art" is a superficial consumer veneer over modernism. It does not completely replace modernism, it is a faith that replaces rationalism only when rationalism has temporarily reached its limit of effectiveness. Modernism is seen as the core perspective over which faith is a veneer.

The movement is part of a response to the failure of the Modernist Avant-Garde. It is an appeal to Divine Intervention to overcome moral oppression. The Divine Intervention is through the purchasing, consumption and creative rearrangement of religious rituals, beliefs and artefacts.

The theology is "a communal practice of creative religious consumerism". There is no central belief other than in the structure of the constant creation of new combinations of religions in a semi-ironic hope that Divine Intervention will occur.

Term defined in MA Thesis "What are the possibilities for Postmodern Religious Art" by Anthony Padgett 2003. It was an analysis of works begun by Padgett since 2002 http://www.theism.co.uk

Final Essay (2005)

Essay 10.

TRIBUNAL QUESTIONNAIRE

1.2 TREATMENT

Main Example

Further to my application of 25 July 2005 to Catherine Wood (Curator of Contemporary Art & Performance), Stuart Comer (Curator of Film and Live Events), at Tate Modern, under the leadership of Sir Nicholas Serota (Director), rejected in a letter from Wood on 7/9/5.

"Re: Sir Henry Tate's Memorial Made of Sugar Cubes -
Performance at Tate Modern

I would like to put in writing my recent proposal to Catherine Wood re performance around the themes of contemporary art and religious fundamentalism. Points 1 & 2 give the rationale behind the proposal, 3 is a sketch of the proposal and 4 is my background.

1. Religion, democracy and fundamentalism will now be a focal point of discussion for the foreseeable future. Religious extremism replaces the Avant Garde as the oppositional force to consumer globalisation. Thus art needs to address issues of religion to remain contemporary.

2. Tate galleries was created by Sir Henry Tate, an active Unitarian (see enclosed information). Unitarianism influenced US constitution and Thomas Jefferson's separation of Church and State, the US provides the prime model of consumer democracy and so Unitarianism provides a model for a liberal "pick n mix" religious democracy.

3. Resurrection of these concerns in a postmodern consumer context can be symbolically achieved through a performance around a reconstruction of Tate Memorial (Norwood Cemetery), in Tate Modern. This would be made of Tate & Lyle sugar cubes at ½ scale. Measured drawings would be on display with the construction. A performance and talk around the work would also occur.

4. I am an artist (and am a Unitarian) and the pioneer of pick n mix religious art with the academic term "postmodern religious art" (subject of my MA thesis and talk at Tate Modern conference "Heaven on Earth" January 2005). My background is in contemporary art, writing, teaching Religious Education, conservation of places of worship for the Palestinian, Israeli and US governments.

I would be very happy to come to London to discuss this proposal in depth with you."

And follow up letter of 25 August 2005

"Re: - Performance at Tate Modern – Request of Response

Further to my letter of 25 July 2005 I would like to request a response.

If you are interested to meet me to discuss my work with a view to putting on a performance, talk, workshop or exhibition then I would be delighted to come to a meeting in London.

If you are not interested in showing my work then please would you respond by letter to this effect – with a statement of why my work is unsuitable (particularly in light of the points of relevance that I raise in my letter of 25 July 2005).

Please would you also return my DVD "Religion Cabaret", held since 30th January 2005, which I understand may have been passed between you."

The main subject of this complaint is my rejection for this proposal. The immediate circumstances leading up to the treatment are as follows:

I gave a talk on "Postmodern Religious Art" at Tate Modern for the Heaven on Earth conference, 27-29 January 2005, organised by the London Consortium in collaboration with the Tate. Stuart Comer chaired the opening discussion 27/1/5 with two artists, Bjorn Melhus and Matthieu Laurette. Comer questioned them about religion and they could not answer. This was an issue he felt was of relevance and one I speak brilliantly on.

Unfortunately he didn't come to my talk 28/1/5 so I left him my "Religion Cabaret" DVD to watch and a list of slides from my talk. I phoned a number of times and 6 months later he still had not watched the film. I took the opportunity to then make a performance proposal to him, Sir Nicholas Serota and Catherine Wood (Curator of Performance). This proposal was open to negotiation and its sketch form was the reawakening of issues around interreligious and artistic expression. The specific form was a performance around a scale reconstruction of the Memorial of Sir Henry Tate, built out of sugar cubes. This would connect the Tate back to issues of history, Unitarianism and current models of art and religion. It was described as reintroducing issues around religion to the Tate. This proposal was rejected and I was not even asked to come for an interview to elaborate on the ideas.

Despite my letters, staff at the Tate have consistently failed to provide me with explanations for their actions and decisions – even when such explanation has been specifically requested in my letter.

Previous Examples

Further circumstances leading up to the treatment are as follows. These may no longer be subject to redress (and many occurred prior to the Regulations) but they show my status as an artist of originality and foresight, who has been unfairly treated. They also show how my work has prefigured the Regulations and current religious climate.

The first major instance of discrimination was with Tate curator Heidi Reitmaier (Curator of Public Programmes) promoting the on-line Tate commissioned work of Shilpa Gupta "Blessed-bandwidth.net" (November 2003) and ignoring my own work -

which was similar but came earlier. In her article "God, Prayer and Politics: The Work of Shilpa Gupta" on the Tate website, Reitmaier promoted Gupta's work as relevant because of its interreligious content and use of technology.

I had already been making interreligious art since 1994, had worked at Holy Sites making art work since 1996, had been involved in technology/religion areas with computer manufactured Muslims 1996-1999, a £150,000 sponsored computer manufactured Seraphim 1999/2000, interactive installations 1999, webcasting 1999, computer generated Muslim/Hindu prints 2001, interactive DVDs 2002, and published articles on this theme "Reconciling Binary Oppositions" in Body, Space and Technology Journal Vol 2 No 1, Brunel 2001 and "Digital Spirituality" in Intersections and Connections – Art and Techonolgy, Springer 2002. Gupta was commissioned to create internet art but the importance was given to the interreligious element of her work, an element I had been exploring, in a more radical fashion since 2002, in Interreligious games, music, fashion, prayer, ritual, sculpture and performance. I had promoted these and subsequent events at the time to Tate curators and at Tate events.

Whilst Gupta had a semi-ironic worship I had created a semi-ironic Interreligious Messiah 2002, given academic papers on this theme and in my first MA thesis on Postmodern Religious Art, October 2003, I explored this issue. My work also went much further relating to issues of commodification and consumerism and the link between sacred and secular. Gupta didn't creatively mix the religions, keeping them in their boxes instead. I mixed different religions with secular culture before Gupta's work. Of importance is that my work is also a genuine religious position and not just an artistic construct.

Primacy of artistic contribution is an industry standard but Tate refused to honour this in my case. Despite my complaints to Vincente Todoli (Director of Tate Britain)17/11/3 and reply by Jemima Rellie (Head of Digital Programmes) and follow-up letter to Todoli, Rellie, Reitmaier and Gregor Muir (Curator) 13/3/4 her work was given preferential treatment and I had no redress on the website.

As well as these factors, the appropriateness of my background (in teaching Religious Education, being involved in interfaith work and working as a historic stonework conservator for both the Israeli and Palestinian Governments) was not taken into consideration.

The second major instance of discrimination that I wrote a letter of complaint about was when Tate Liverpool had the "Seeing is Believing" exhibition 11 December 2004 to 2 May 2005, on art relating to different religions to coincide with Liverpool Capital of Culture Theme of "Faith in One City". I had already contacted the organisers of the Capital of Culture about my work being appropriate to "Faith in One City" and they advised me to exhibit as part of Liverpool Biennial, where I exhibited "Divinityland" (Interreligious Themepark in Liverpool's Quaker Meeting House) put on a Religion Cabaret (Magnet Bar) and presenting an Interreligious wedding cake at opening events of the Biennial (Independents).

"Seeing is Believing" occurred after Liverpool Biennial and before it began I contacted Amy Dickson, the curator, about exhibiting my work. She did not come to my exhibition and said I could not show any work, as it was not in the collection. My work was more progressive than any shown and should have been recognised as such and purchased for the collection.

The lack of contemporary relevance of "Seeing is Believing" was noted in Waldemar Januszczak's article for the Sunday Times "We need religious art more than ever, says Waldemar Januszczak – but his spirit wasn't revived by Tate Liverpool's Seeing is Believing". My work would have provided this. I wrote to Sir Nicholas Serota concerning this 20/12/4 who replied 21/2/5 that he passed my letter to the Tate's Collections division. They did not reply to me.

Other instances occurred where I promoted my work to the Tate but was ignored, even though my work was ahead. In 2002 the Rev Ethan Acres performed at the Tate Modern Turbine Hall and explored the cross-over of consumerism and religion. His work was limited to a largely Christian perspective (with undertones of Contemporary art spirituality) and although I had already exhibited an interreligious fashion show and disco in the Arts Café, London, E1(2002) exploring some of these issues, I was ignored.

My 2003 contemporary art exhibition Stop Armageddon/Garden of Eden at the Quaker Gallery just of Trafalgar Square came before Damien Hirst's "In-A-Gadda-Da-Vida" (in the Garden of Eden exhibition at the Tate 2004). I wrote a letter of complaint to Reitmaier 8/1/4 concerning the lack of Tate interest in my work but received no real answer. The Utopian work and the interreligious games (board games, scalextric and fruit-machine) I created 2002-3 were also followed by the Common Wealth 22 October to 28 December 2003 exhibitions at Tate around ideas of Utopian art and games in contemporary art.

Rietmaier also chaired a Symposium "Tool versus Meduim. The Use of Rapid Prototyping in Contemporary Sculpture" at De Montfort University in Autumn 2004 but despite my writing to her 19/7/4 , and her previously being notified, about my award winning Rapid Prototype Sculptures (with religious themes) dating back to 1998, she did not reply. I also approached to the Tate Galleries Education Department to work with them on cross-curricular art and religion projects but received no reply.

Finally, my suggestions 16/4/4 to the Tate of an "inventory of originality" for artists to register works was rejected by Rellie following a letter sent to Reitmaier, Todoli and Muir. This seems easily achievable by data base forms and would provide much needed accountability for original contributions and ensure equal opportunities and non-discriminatory practice.

1.3 UNLAWFUL DISCRIMINATION

Direct And Indirect Discrimination

I believe that I am the subject of religious discrimination according to The Employment Equality (Religion or Belief) Regulations 2003.

The reasons for discrimination may not be understood initially by staff at Tate Modern and this is because discriminatory practices are often the result of lack of understanding and lack of a desire to understand. This treatment of the other as strange and not worthy of proper consideration is discriminatory and as the form and content of my work is of a religious nature it is therefore religious discrimination.

I have given the Tate an opportunity to take positive action over issues of religion and religious discrimination in artwork and it has rejected this. This shows an non-acceptance of the significance of these issues and is further evidence of its discriminatory position.

My work is a celebration of the Regulations and the Tate's unwillingness to take my work seriously is a contravention of the Regulations.

As well as being subject to direct discrimination from Tate curators, I have also been subject to further, indirect discrimination.

Tate takes its cues from the worlds of commercial art, state art and the mainstream media – all of which currently operate levels of religious discrimination. This institutional discrimination is like institutional racism, only against religious believers. Art is not just about money but about religious values as well. I argue that it is the job of the Tate Curators, Director and Trustees, as guardians of the public interest, to determine what is of significance and relevance in contemporary art in Britain and internationally. This means that they should apply The Employment Equality (Religion and Belief) Regulations 2003 to the world of contemporary art – ensuring that the art business does not operate solely for financial ends and that public galleries implement correct policy.

This indirect discrimination has also prevented me from access to opportunities to do works in galleries and media that will reach a larger audience.

Merit of my Work

The Acquisitions Policy states that "In the field of contemporary art, acquisitions reflect those artists who have already made a significant contribution and have achieved national or international recognitions. Potential acquisitions of contemporary art generally come from artist's dealers, other commercial galleries or collectors."

PMRA is a term I have coined for an art movement that I have pioneered. It is the subject of my MA Thesis "What are the possibilities for Postmodern Religious Art and Peformance?" (Wimbledon School of Art). This new and unique contribution to art (where I show how religious equality principles apply to contemporary art) was prior to, and went beyond, the work of Tate commissioned Shilpa Gupta and Tate Liverpool's faith exhibition.

My work has been nationally recognised, being the subject of debates on BBC Radio 4, TES and the Mail on Sunday. My television program ideas have been used for the Channel 4 program "Spirituality Shopper" and my articles have been published.

My work has been internationally recognised, winning the About Vision international art and technology competition in 2002, being in the finals of the International Jewish Artist of the Year Awards 2004, being part of the Polish Castle of Imagination Live Art Festival 2004, being in a panel talk at New York Studio School, printed in the Belgian Q Magazine and being reviewed at Edinburgh Fringe.

My gallery talk (6/1/5) for the international ICA exhibition "100 Artists See God" illustrated how advanced my conceptual work was (over the current practice of the 100 artists invited in 2003 to take part in the exhibition and over the curators' approach to the subject).

The quality of my work is excellent and ground-breaking. Whilst these credits may not be sufficient for Tate to consider my work to be of national and international significance this is because of indirect discrimination.

Without discrimination I would have been able to make large scale works. Prejudice against religion in the art-world has meant, through lack of financial support, my works have been restricted in size and venues exhibited in, but this does not change the conceptual merit of my work.

The prime feature of my work is conceptual, although the quality of many of my works is exceptional in many of the mediums I have experimented with I am less concerned with the issue of quality than with concept. This is part because I am responding in my work to artistic notions of the ready-made and the scatological, so quality is not necessary.

Religion or Art

Although I have been discriminated against on the basis of religion this does not mean that my work is solely religious and is not art. It is a combination of the 2. That my work has a religious approach and content does not mean that it belongs to a religious venue and not an art gallery. I argue that religion is more important than art but this doesn't invalidate my work as being art. The important fact is that artistic thinking affects my thinking about religion so that the result is a hybrid of the two. Art that just illustrates religion is not art, just illustration. The religious content needs to challenge the very nature of art and the artistic content needs to challenge the very nature of religion. My art is primarily conceptual about the nature of religion and about the religious nature of contemporary art.

Art should be open to an exploration of religion and I show why art and religion are not absolutist and that a mixing with other religions and beliefs characterises a postmodern age. No one has created work around this theme (and taken it to its logical conclusions) apart from myself.

Postmodern Religious Art (PMRA)

My religion is serious, cohesive, and cogent and was the subject of my MA Thesis. My art has not been given a fair hearing because of discrimination against my general religious views Postmodern Religious Art (PMRA) and their particular instantiation as Disco Art Religion (DAR). This has stopped the Tate from looking at my ideas (of PMRA) and they have confused the religious content of PMRA as being just religious work, rather than art ideas about the relation between religion and art. Just as with all ideas of art –PMRA is a new concept and is therefore art.

PMRA is a superficial, creative, pick n mix, consumerism of religions and beliefs. It is a semi-ironic means to divine intervention. It is also a campaign for the rights of individual religious freedoms (against atheistic and religious extremism) using modernist liberal political structures. The demonstration of the application of this belief is shown here, in my potentially taking Tate galleries to the Employment Tribunal. Even this very case is a piece of artwork, where I am expanding the definitions of art (and religion). PMRA, however, is not primarily a political movement.

PMRA unites people, not through a shared, deeper spirituality but through superficial religious items. The work is "plastic" but with a hope that something genuine can come through. The majority of people operate mainly on a superficial level and not on a deep level, so I take the superficial items of division and put them all together in order to make a unity. The unity is through people being creative consumers of superficial religion. My work is not about finding the common core, it is about finding the bits that divide people and uniting those bits to create unity between people.

In my MA Thesis I argue that the superficial, physical forms of various religious traditions are more relevant to artistic production than the deeper spiritual elements of most artists in the Tate collection, eg Bill Viola, Anish Kapoor and Anthony Gormley.

The Regulations do not equate religious belief such superficial manifestation of belief (eg clothing, prayer or ritual). However, my belief is that the superficial manifestations have a deeper power – it is not the superficial manifestations alone, but the belief attached to them.

The Regulations recognise that religious traditions do not always have the same practices, nor are these always followed in the same way, nor are all of these practices necessarily followed. I further adapt this into pick and mix religion, that also mixes with secular culture. Because of the genuine faith element of my art my work constitutes a religious position.

The discrimination is that the Tate curators are not prepared to look at my ideas of PMRA because they discriminate against my religion. Rejection of anything concerning religion is endemic in the art-world and the curators are also following indirect discriminatory practice.

I show in my MA thesis how in PMRA I take art forwards but the Tate curators do not even entertain this possibility because of the religious content of the work.

Genuine Occupational Requirement (GOR) and the Religious Bias of Tate Modern/Contemporary Art

A number of assumptions are made concerning the nature of art and religion when curators make decisions. These belief assumptions are part of the Genuine Occupational Requirement (GOR) curators apply. The Tate takes its cue from commercial galleries where this basis for GOR is present but it is also prevalent in educational establishments, international art fairs (largely commercial) and state funded art programs.

The Tate is part of a contemporary art-world that has a religious/belief bias (as its GOR) that is unjustifiable and discriminates against my own position. The position that it holds is largely based in "critical thinking", atheism, spiritualism, pantheism, the "everyday", liminality, scatological gnosticism and quasi-socialism. Religion is largely rejected on Marxist based political grounds. This contradicts the Regulations, unless it can be demonstrated that this rejection is essential to a GOR.

In my MA Thesis I show why a focus purely on aesthetics and aesthetic innovation leads to a purely formal view that has mystical and spiritual consequences that can be associated with Eastern Religions and Modern art. I articulate the religious position that is Postmodern and not a pre-modern religious view that modern art reacts against. I also argue that the content that is allowed in contemporary art is also largely atheistic, modernist, spiritual or ironically/negatively religious.

In Art Theory many thinkers now reject the efficacy of critical thinking and socialism (eg. Bonito Oliva, Achille. "Trans-Avantgarde International" Mil., 1982 or Jameson, Frederick "Postmodernism, or the Cultural Logic of Late Capitalism" Verso, 1991) so there can no longer be a reason to accept a socialist rejection of religion. PMRA moves on from this as the failure of political thinking in art is rejected in favour of a belief in the political consequences of treating Religion in a radically artistic manner. These political consequences of my art may even be seen in these Discrimination proceedings. My work, however, is not primarily political, rather I put faith in Divine Intervention.

An alternative political move against power structures is made by art theorists in their focus on the everyday and the scatological (by trying to level ideas of hierarchy). In my thesis I demonstrate how this artistic consciousness again relates to modernist mysticism. To add to this bias Contemporary art also has a particular spiritual/religious bias towards Eastern, mystical, non-dualistic thinking.

Texts (such as Taylor, Mark C. "Disfiguring: Art, Architecture, Religion" University of Chicago Press 1992, Baas, Jacquelynn "Buddha Mind in Contemporary Art", University of California Press 2004 , Elkins, James "On the Strange Place of Religion in Contemporary Art" Routledge 2004, etc etc) show a spiritual basis in art that rejects treating Monotheistic religion seriously or sympathetically.

There are some exceptions to this rejection, such as work by Mark Wallinger, but these tend to be mainly Christian or to be based in a mystical Gnostic self-mortification eg Heartney, Eleanor

"Postmodern Heretics: Catholic Imagination in Contemporary Art" Midmarch Arts Press 2004. Contemporary Christian Art, accepted by the Tate, consists mainly of works that criticise religion, such as those by Damien Hirst and Sarah Lucas, or relate to full irony.

Other religious views are largely absent. Kutlug Ataman's "Twelve" (2004) in last years Turner Prize explored issues of reincarnation but the religious aspect of the subject was kept to a minimum. The focus being on the identity, histories and language of the interviewees, rather than on their Muslim backgrounds.

Art that is positive about religion is generally rejected and vastly unrepresented in the art world. At best, a space of openness is left for the viewer to decide for themselves see Tom Lubbock's article 'Entertaining the Unbelievable' in "Modern Painters" Spring 2004. In my MA thesis I argue that this openness is a liminality with particular religious, mystical, non-dualistic implications.

Galleries show art works from major religions but where it is represented it tends to illustrate the artwork and is just a concept to hang a piece of artwork upon. There is no real interaction to the art form and the art-form does not change the religion in any substantial way. Any work that has the appearance of being from a genuine cult is rejected, unless the work or cult is fully ironic. My work is a genuine investigation of the cross-over between religion and contemporary art. Categorising it as a weird cult is prejudicial to both myself and to other cults/sects/movements.

PMRA vs GOR

PMRA is as legitimate a belief as the one currently held in the GOR of contemporary art, but as it is outside the current GOR belief it has not been given time and an opportunity for a fair hearing. Without a fair hearing people cannot appreciate the ground-breaking significance and originality of my contribution to art with PMRA.

Artists have a role to break away from fixed beliefs and a GOR belief should not be a standard with which to prejudge work. The Tate should not refuse my work because it doesn't fit with current art ideas. My beliefs should not be seen as conflicting with the

Tate's GOR belief, which should be open to adaptation and new beliefs.

I argue and demonstrate how the current contemporary art GOR belief is outdated, in comparison with my own, in my MA thesis. My argument is not the crude assertion that art should be under the authority of religion but rather that art cannot avoid being under religion's authority. I pose the problem, that by rejecting religion that art adopts a religious position. Thus questioning openly how they can discriminate against religions when their very system of choice is religious.

My position is more appropriate to the Tate than their current viewpoint. Tate curators have taken on the religious viewpoints endemic in contemporary art and my work is closer to notions of artistic creativity. I change the nature of art rather than stay with the GOR belief, therefore only I am truly contemporary, and closer to the correct Tate Ethos.

Original Tate Ethos

Sir Henry Tate did not state conditions in his original bequest but isn't the fact that he was a Unitarian (and donated to many Unitarian causes) interesting, relevant and worth exploring by the Tate galleries in the current cultural climate? Whilst public funds should not serve a religious affiliation, Sir Henry Tate's religion coincides with current Equal Opportunities policies – ie liberal democracy. Unitarian support of liberal principles of free thinking and individual conscience was held as being a light for equal opportunities through the 19th-20th centuries. Shouldn't this be represented somewhere by the Tate?

Would this be illegal religious discrimination in favour of Unitarianism? No, if the Tate must promote a view it is better to promote one in line with the Regulations than the one in its current GOR. Unitarianism is a religion/viewpoint with an Ethos that is very close to the Regulations.

Religious Discrimination Act

Unitarianism is an example of the Religion Bill in applying equally to all religious and non-religious viewpoints.

In line with the Regulations Unitarianism rejects any form of discrimination and promotes all to become ministers regardless of gender, sexual orientation, race and also promotes same sex marriage. Unitarianism also allows people of other religions eg. Muslim or Jewish Unitarian, to be members.

Unitarianism both is a "liberal religious" position that is both religious and is not religious – just like the Regulations.

The Regulations and Unitarianism give a meta-view, ie they concerns religions and are not necessarily religious themselves. In this sense they are non-religious. This has been the perspective of Unitarians since the 19th century, that a meta-view (of freedom, rationality, respect, openness, diversity) unites them in their search for religious, artistic or scientific truths. Unitarians can have any belief – even atheistic or Trinitarian – as the important element is common unity through respecting the rights of individuals.

Unitarianism is a meta-religious positions that helps people choose their own religious positions/truths. The Regulations also have implications of tolerance and acceptance that contradict some of the more extreme interpretations of religions. The Regulations are therefore religious in their position as to what can constitute a valid religion. Just like Unitarianism, the Regulations are a position that is both religious and not religious.

This is demonstrated in the way that the Regulations do not change the nature of Unitarianism whereas, in contrast, other general religious viewpoints (such as Christianity, Islam, Judaism, Contemporary Art etc) are changed into more liberal versions by the Regulations.

PMRA is also a meta-structure whereby many Unitarian principles are expanded along lines of contemporary art. I am the founder of that artistic structure/concept (that facilitates individuals' formulations of religious truths). The particular religion that I manifest out of PMRA is DAR and my particular manifestations of PMRA are important because they are the first ever instantiation of that meta-structure.

The Regulations are both general principles of the current liberal ideology and have elements of a general religious/belief system. Unitarianism is both close to the current liberal ideology and a religion, PMRA is both an artistic view and a religion.

The difference between the Regulations, Unitarianism and PMRA is that whilst all 3 maintain liberal meta-perspectives on religion, when they are put into application the Regulations are a general set of ethical rules and beliefs (that have consequences in curtailing the specific beliefs of others) whereas Unitarianism and PMRA are specific and individual creations of ethical rules and beliefs.

Both Unitarianism and PMRA are non-religious meta-beliefs as well as religious beliefs. Issues of my belief were not appropriate to my application to the Tate (other than to show that I practice my beliefs as well as have a meta-position). Discrimination has occurred against me and my work as it has been treated as a belief only, without looking at its deeper implications.

A person's religion can be positively discriminated in favour of them getting a job, but cannot then be a part of the job unless a GOR. Gupta's standard, non-religious, art views may have allowed her to get employment to make a non-committed work about religion. If artists have a GOR belief then Gupta's adherence to it can have secured her the position.

Gupta is a precedent to say interreligious work is of merit but is promoted by the Tate because the content does not present a genuine religious belief, just a meta-view. Her work gives a structure for people to choose religions from and does not show her own choices. Gupta lets people choose a particular religion but is not mixing any of them. The mode of worship is not new (internet) because it is used by other online religious communities. What is new is that she provides religious options for this mode of worship.

The GOR, however, should be open to maximum freedom of expression adding a significant new contribution to art. Unlike my own work there is no indication that Gupta's is part of a real religious system. This work doesn't artistically challenge notions of religion, therefore is a lesser work than my own.

In art, perhaps religion could be part of the job if the artwork commission is about a person's experience of a particular religion. At "Seeing is Believing" the Tate showed religious art by members of the religious groups the art was about, or by artists from the community that these religions were in. My lack of a single traditional religious position would not exclude me as my work is about superficial consumerism of religion and I am from that group (of superficial consumers). However, if the work is about religion would this just be content of the artwork and not a formal innovation, and therefore not art?

My work is a formal innovation as it is conceptual art that shows why content is important; by my arguing that contemporary art, and even purely formal art, has a religious basis to it. In deconstructing contemporary art I can expand the GOR belief and free art to apply to religious thinking and the nature of belief. My medium is the nature of religious belief and my innovation is the artistic perspective of PMRA – a superficial consumerism of religion/belief options with a hope and a semi-ironic faith that this will lead to divine interventions. This is built over a layer of Modernist political structures and formal art systems and methods.

Tate accepted Gupta's work about belief structures, but my work has been ignored. My work was earlier, has greater options and implications and also has a working example of the religion. The religious content (DAR being a practising religion) of my work is important because it is the first instantiation of PMRA. Gupta's work is a meta-view in line with the Regulations, but it is not artistically progressive over the Regulations, nor does it show the application of the meta-view. PMRA is progressive over the Regulations and I show the application of its meta-view with DAR. My work is not just about religion, it is a religion.

Perhaps the Tate should have encouraged my application as a follower of the Regulations and a minority religion (religious aspect of PMRA) against the prevailing GOR belief but select my work based upon my artistic merit (founder of the non-religious aspect of PMRA) without discrimination (positive or negative) with regards to my religion (PMRA & DAR).

I think the Tate has been discriminatory against DAR and also the religious content of PMRA (not realising how close the position is to the Regulations). As the Tate has discriminated against my religion (PMRA & DAR) it does not recognise my merits (of being the founder of the PMRA perspective). I also think that they have discriminated against my Unitarianism by rejecting its relation to the Regulations and have not taken seriously the implications of the Regulations for Tate.

Acquistions

The current acquisition policy is too general to prevent discriminatory practices from occurring and as a result the acquisitions policy at the Tate is indirectly discriminatory against religion.

Commercial and non-religious criteria should not be imposed that have the effect of discriminating against people who have artistic work of significant national and international merit (such as my own).

Why does the Tate consult commercial galleries for its acquisitions but doesn't ask religious groups in general for advice on acquisitions? This is a very discriminatory bias in itself from a state funded gallery. If there is current uncertainty about whether religious groups should do this then Tate should welcome an approach that can throw light on issues of Religion. The Tate method of determining artistic merit is limited in scope and should welcome PMRA, an expansive way of thinking about the involvement of religion that is also a new way of making art.

My art skills and conceptual art skills are clear. What is not is the recognition by commercial galleries. However the Tate is a public funded gallery and should not apply solely commercial considerations or be led by commercial bodies. The Regulations even advise a company (like Tate) to make small financial loss in order to ensure non-discrimination.

Curators should suspect that my work would be discriminated against by commercial galleries and institutions with the GOR belief of contemporary art. Taking on just the views of commercial or public funded GOR galleries constitutes indirect discrimination by curators. Business would be the principal model if art was completely business focussed, but it is not.

Curatorial discrimination should be prevented in acquisitions considerations and positive action should be taken against the culture of discrimination that was prejudiced against my work. That any such discrimination by curators may have been inadvertent or accidental is not an excuse. It is still unlawful. Discrimination often occurs when people are unaware that they are being discriminatory. They can also be unaware of holding mistaken GOR beliefs that can be used prejudicially. The benefits of PMRA cannot be seen by curators as it has not been entertained due to discrimination.

The individual merits of various artists should be assessed, regardless of their religious focus. Business gallery beliefs, and GOR beliefs cannot be used as a justification for continued discrimination against me. The issues that I raise in this letter must be answered fully by the Tate, without recourse to assumptions and prejudice.

My quality of work is clear because I have introduced a completely new and revolutionary perspective in art. I coined the term PMRA in 2003 and it refers to both real art and real religion.

Aims of the Tate

As the Tate Board determines policy they are responsible for ensuring that there is no Religious Discrimination in policy documents (including discrimination by omission). They also decide on major acquisitions and are guardians of public interest. As they are required by the Museums and Galleries Act 1992 to extend the awareness, understanding and appreciation of British art and international modern and contemporary art then groundbreaking art of an interreligious nature would fit all these categories. The board are advised to think carefully on this matter and the effect that the Regulations have on the objectives of the Tate.

Some of the Aims of the Tate are stated in the Accounts 2003-2004 as being; to strengthen and extend the range of the Tate's Collection and the intellectual assets surrounding it, to put on innovative displays, develop more diverse audiences and to develop the Tate's role in the wider world. All of these would be enhanced by the inclusion of PMRA and are compromised by its rejection. The strategy for the Tate doesn't make mention of Religion or religious issues. Despite my drawing attention to the significance of these issues to contemporary life, and how my work relates, my proposal was still rejected.

Should the fact that Britain is mainly Christian, Atheist and Humanist be a factor that can influence acquisition choices for British Art? The collection also relates to international art, so the religious make-up of the international community should also be considered. These and related issues need to be put into the policy statements of theTate.

Although there is now legislation in place to prevent religious discrimination, Trustees could have a conflict of religious interest. Trustees need to declare any financial conflict of interest, so should they also declare any conflict of religious interest – to help them avoid discriminating in favour of a particular belief?

In order to help the Tate Trustees to comply with the Regulations there should be Religious advisors on the Board, as well as advisers from commercial galleries, as art relates to the spiritual and moral health of the nation.

The Accounts 2003-2004 mentions "Employee involvement and disabled persons" but makes no mention of the Regulations that came into effect in 2003 and how the Tate would try and comply for employees and visitors.

Employment

The Regulations apply to both private and public sector recruitment for any size business.

An acquisition from an artist is a form of employment. A financial deal over work and services done in providing a piece of artwork.

Tate has an open tender process and curators can select submitted work that is of interest to the Tate criteria of acquisition. The submission of works for purchase, exhibition or performance is an application for employment and would involve a contract (written or verbal).

As a potential self-employed contractor I was seeking a personal contract with Tate galleries. The self-employment would be a contract even if not described as such in the application.

The initial employers are seen as the curators at Tate galleries, but the main employer is seen as Sir Nicholas Serota, who is accountable to Trustees.

The Trustees may also have inadvertently continued a culture of religious discrimination. Just as galleries can negatively influence the decision of curators the Trustees can negatively influence the decision of Serota. If Curators and Serota are influenced then this is also indirect discrimination. Presumably Serota is liable for curators as their "employer".

Offensive

Perhaps the Tate rejected my work because it was deemed offensive to faith groups. My work cannot be rejected due to this for the following reasons:

My work is a genuine artistic and religious expression. The history, power or size of a traditional religion is no reason to allow its believers to harass me over my freedom of expression. All these religions were originally new, small and differed to the older religions around them.

Artistic precedents have been set with derogatory/offensive work about Christianity, such as Andre Serrano's "Piss Christ" (1987). My work is less offensive than much of this and is less discriminatory against Christianity as it applies to all religions.

I am not harassing religions or degrading them, rather I am exploring issues of art and religious history, eg. my creation of the Rainbow Swastika may be seen as a reason why my work is too controversial. However, this would be a prejudicial statement that does not look at the religious and intellectual reasons for my using the symbol. I have shown this work extensively, including at the Ben Uri (Jewish Contemporary Art) gallery, at Limmudfest (a Jewish festival), at Edinburgh Fringe (favourably reviewed in the Jewish Telegraph) and on Channel 5 to name a few.

The work is intended to create a humorous, peaceful and fun environment. This is designed to increase dignity and tolerance and reject bigotry and intolerance. Dignity could be defined as the ability to laugh at oneself rather than react violently. My work is positive towards religions and playful so who sees it as offensive, perhaps they are being vexatious and offensive themselves. If someone feels offended or harassed they have to show not just their feeling of being harassed but also that it was reasonable to react/feel in that way.

All faiths contain hateful statements towards other faiths. The reason that they now co-operate is through liberalisation, which my art is part of the process of (and which is part of the tradition that the Regulations also come from).

The Times Educational Supplement 25/2/5 quoted Rupert Kaye, the chief executive of the Association of Christian Teachers as saying that my "Divinityland" schools' workshop was "demeaning to the faiths" but TES misrepresented my work to faith leaders and the issues it raises around liberalism, and it is this liberalism that has led to the Regulation in the first place. It is interesting to note that TES also quoted Mr Kaye as saying "If this were in the Tate Modern I would take it with a pinch of salt..." implying he could easily imagine it being at Tate Modern.

Justification

The Tate needs to show why it has not behaved in a discriminatory and prejudicial manner.

The Tate must now show why they considered my work and ideas to be invalid. If the Tate does not agree with my arguments herein they must prove why my work and ideas are invalid.

The Tate must show how my work does not fit their GOR "belief" (contemporary arts theory). My having different views on art is not reason to reject me from an application for the job.

I am not looking for favourable treatment, just treatment in line with a recognition of my contribution to contemporary art.

Compensation

As compensation I would like to be one of the 4 shortlisted nominees for the 2006 Turner Prize. As the prize is for works from the previous year I would like to be nominated for making this complaint – and expanding the concepts and roles of art, religion and galleries.

This is not the reason that I have made this complaint, my reason is because I believe that I have been religiously discriminated against. This is a suggestion for compensation appropriate to the level of discrimination.

Not accepting the seriousness of my being shortlisted is a further example of discrimination and not having considered my work fairly.

I would like an opportunity to show my work, not as a peripheral event but as a proper exhibition given the weight that my work is due.

The selecting Jury is made of various figures from the world of contemporary art. Ensuring that the Jury shortlist my work would compensate both for direct discrimination from the Tate and for their indirect discrimination by accepting a culture of religious discrimination in the world of contemporary art.

I hope that you will recognise that you (Tate) have been discriminatory and that we can resolve this matter without recourse to Employment Tribunal.

4. OTHER QUESTIONS

As well as answering questions concerning application of the Regulations I would like an answer from the Tate over the following.

Why doesn't my religious work fit their current acquisitions criteria? The Tate must show how my work does not fit their GOR "belief" (contemporary arts theory).

Does Tate have a religious ethos or religious policy?

Does the Tate have issues of Equality and Religious Discrimination written into its acquisitions policy?

How do the Regulations fit with their current criteria?

How do they think their criteria should be adjusted to comply with the Regulations?

Do they think my work will, or will not, fit a fully compliant criteria?

Why does the Tate consult commercial galleries for its acquisitions but doesn't ask religious groups in general for advice on acquisitions?

What are the religious/belief views of Sir Nicholas Serota and the Board of Trustees at the Tate (particularly with regards to fundamental assumptions about art)?

What are the religious beliefs of Curators at the Tate, and what are their attitudes towards religion.

What are the religious beliefs of the artists whose work is shown at the Tate, and what are their attitudes towards religion

What is the religious make up of the staff at Tate Galleries.

What are the religious beliefs of visitors to the Tate Galleries.

What was the Tate's perception of my Religious beliefs at the time of my application?

What provision for, and application of, the new Regulations have been made?

Are the Regulations written into Tate Equal Opportunities documents or mission statements?

Are there prayer rooms or places of worship for staff?

Have there been other cases of Religious Discrimination at the Tate?

REFERENCES

Essay 3

1) IV Introduction, *Art in Theory 1900-1990*, p333
2) Brigitte Hanmann, *Hitler's Vienna: A Dictator' Apprenticeship* Oxford University Press 1999, p210
3) Hanmann, ibid p227
4) Hanmann, ibid p78
5) Hanmann, ibid p76
6) Hanmann, ibid p202
7) Katerina Clark and Michael Holquist, Chapter 14 – Rabelais and His World, in *Mikhael Bakhtin*, Harvard College, 1984, pp. 295-320
8) Clark and Holquist, ibid
9) Clark and Holquist, ibid
10) Clark and Holquist, ibid
11) Clark and Holquist, ibid
12) Clark and Holquist, ibid
13) Clark and Holquist, ibid
14) Yve-Alain Bois, "The Use Value of "Formless"", in Bois, Yve-Alain and Rosalind Krauss, *Formless: A User's Guide*, New York (Zone Books), 1997, pp.26
15) Bois, ibid p 17
16) Bois, ibid p30
17) Bois, ibid p37
18) Bois, ibid p32
19) Stallabras, High Art Lite, p3
20) Stallabras, ibid p139
21) Stallabras, ibid p123
22) Stallabras, ibid p99
23) Stallabras, ibid p230
24) Stallabras, ibid p232
25) Stallabras, ibid p230
26) Ralph Rugoff, Fop Art in www.LAweekly.com
27) Stallabras, ibid p280
28) John Roberts, "Domestic Squabbles", in *Who's Afraid of Red, White and Blue?*, p50
29) Stallabras, ibid p210
30) Stallabras, ibid p274
31) Stallabras, ibid p153
32) Douglas Foght, London, February 27, 1995 LAAT
www.vpro.nl/data/laat/materiaal/chapman-bros-interview.shtml
33) Maia Damianovic, *Journal of Contemporary Art* 1997 www.jca-online.com
34) Jan Avgikas, "Gagosian Gallery", *Art Forum International,* vol 36, Dec 1997, p116
35) Rachel Withers, "Exhibit", *Art Forum International,* vol 37, no 4, Dec 1998, p140-1
36) Mark Sladen, "The Body in Question", *Art Monthly,* no 191, 1995
37) Dinos Chapman, "Gender is an Organic Superstition", *MAKE: The Magazine of Womens' Art,* Aug/Sept 1996, p18-9

38) Robert Rosenblum, Dinos Chapman and Jake Chapman, Gagosian Gallery, *Unholy Libel,* 1997

39) Rosenblum, Chapman and Chapman, ibid

40) Rosenblum, Chapman and Chapman, ibid

41) David Falconer, "Doctorin' the Retardis" in *Chapmanworld*

42) Falconer, ibid

43) Falconer, ibid

44) Falconer, ibid

45) Douglas Fogle, "A Scatological Aesthetics for the Tired of Seeing" in *Chapmanworld,*

46) Fogle, ibid

47) Falconer, ibid

48) Eleanor Heartney, "New York Exhibit", *Art in America,* vol 85, Nov 1997, p120

49) Martyn Maloney, "The Chapman Brothers", *Flash Art* (International Edition), no 186, Jan/Feb 1996, p64-7

50) Stallabras, ibid p147

51) Martha Schwendener, "Gagosian", *New Art Examiner*, vol 25, Dec 97/Jan 98, p46

52) Schwendener, ibid p46

53) Neal Brown, "Victoria Miro Gallery", *Art and Text,* no 50, Jan 1995, p74

54) Stallabras, ibid p147

55) Stallabras, ibid p88

56) Stallabras, ibid p208

57) Rosenblum, Chapman and Chapman, ibid p

58) Lyn Barber, "Brothers in Art", *Observer,* 1999

59) Laurie Attias, "Galerie Templon", *Sculpture* (Washington D.C.), vol 17, no 9, Nov 1998, p76

60) Stallabras, ibid p140

61) Stallabras, ibid p122

62) Stallabras, ibid p101

63) Jonathan Jones, *Frieze* 1999 Issue 47

Essay 4

1) Artaud, Antonin, "Two Letters on Cruelty" in *The Theater and its Double*, trans Corti, Victor, Calder Publications, 1999

2) Artaud, Antonin, "An Affective Athleticism" in *The Theater and its Double*, trans Corti, Victor, Calder Publications, 1999 p92

3) Goodall, Jane *Artaud and the Gnostic Drama* Clarendon Press Oxford 1994 p215

4) Goodall, Op. Cit. p208

5) Goodall, Op. Cit. p208

6) Goodall, Op. Cit. p217

7) Goodall, Op. Cit. p17

8) Goodall, Op. Cit. p4

9) Baker-White, Robert "Artaud's Legacy in the Collectivist Avant-Garde: Community and Representation in Works by Grotowski, Chaikin and Schechner" in *Antonin Artaud and the Modern Theater* Ed. Plunka, Gene A. Associated University Press 1994

10) Artaud, Antonin, "Theatre and Cruelty" in *The Theater and its Double*, trans Corti, Victor, Calder Publications, 1999 p66

11) Baker-White, Op. Cit p202

12) Artaud, Antonin, "Seraphim's Theatre" in *The Theater and its Double*, trans Corti, Victor, Calder Publications, 1999 p101
13) Artaud, Antonin, "The Theatre of Cruelty (First Manifesto)" in *The Theater and its Double*, trans Corti, Victor, Calder Publications, 1999 p76
14) Artaud, Antonin, "An Affective Athleticism" Op.Cit. p90
15) Artaud, Antonin, "An Affective Athleticism" Op. Cit. p95
16) Artaud, Antonin, "Seraphim's Theatre" Op. Cit. p101
17) Baker-White, Op. Cit p205
18) Baker-White, Op. Cit p206
19) Baker-White, Op. Cit p203
20) Artaud, Antonin, "The Theatre of Cruelty (First Manifesto)" Op. Cit. p71-72
21) Artaud, Antonin, "The Theatre of Cruelty (First Manifesto)" Op. Cit. p72
22) Artaud, Antonin, "The Theatre of Cruelty (First Manifesto)" Op. Cit. p77
23) Young, Iris Marion "The Ideal of Community and the Politics of Difference" in *Feminism/Postmodernism* Ed. Nicholson, Linda J. Routledge 1990
24) Young, Op. Cit p309
25) Young, Op. Cit p310
26) Baker-White, Op. Cit p212
27) Baker-White, Op. Cit p213
28) Baker-White, Op. Cit p 218
29) Artaud, Antonin, "Theatre and the Plague" in *The Theater and its Double*, trans Corti, Victor, Calder Publications, 1999 p22
30) http://www.foolishpeople.com
31) http://www.foolishpeople.com

Essay 5

1) Carroll, Pete *The Magick of Chaos* http://www.chaosmatrix.org
2) Clark, David K. & Geisler, Norman L. *Apologetics in the New Age: A Christian Critique of Pantheism* Baker 1990 p228
3) Clark, David K. & Geisler, Norman L. Op. Cit. p228
4) Derrida, Jacques "Faith and Knowledge: The Two Sources of "Religion" at the Limits of Reason Alone" 1996 *Acts of Religion* Routledge 2002 p55
5) Cooper, Cheryl "Aporais of chora" in Hubbard, Sue & Morley, Simon *Chora* Exhibition Booklet 2000
6) Broadhurst, Susan *Liminal Acts: A Critical Overview of Contemporary Performance and Theory* Cassell 2000 p34
7) Broadhurst, Susan Op. Cit. p43
8) Broadhurst, Susan Op. Cit. p31
9) Goldberg, RoseLee *Performance: Live Art since the 60's* Thames and Hudson 1998

Essay 6

1) Nesbit, Molly. Obrist, Hans Ulrich. and Tiravanija, Tirkrit. Meeting Immanueal Wallerstein, "Utopia Station", *50th Venice Biennale exhibition catalogue*, p369
2) Enwezor, Okuwi, "The Black Box", *Documenta XI exhibition catalogue* (2002), p47
3) Levin, Kim. "More Is More" *Village Voice*, November 27, 2002, p64
4) Stallabrass, Julian. *High Art Lite*, Verso 1999, p286

5)Tate Magazine, Issue 3, http://www.tate.org.uk/magazine/issue3/michaellandy.htm

6) Stallabrass, Julian. Op.cit, p75-9

7) Stallabrass, Julian. Op.cit, p75-9

8) Bois, Yve-Alain & Krauss, Rosalind *Formless – A Users Guide* 1997 MIT Press, p252

9) Bois, Yve-Alain & Krauss, Rosalind. Op.cit, p252

10) Fiat, Christopher. "The Experience of Violence in Sacrifice", *Documenta XI exhibition catalogue* (2002)

11) Enwezor, Okuwi, "Interview with Thomas Hirschhorn", *Thomas Hirschhorn: Jumbo Spoons and Big Cake The Art Institute of Chicago World Airport The Renaissance Society at The University of Chicago*, Lowitz + Sons, Chicago, 2000, p29

12) O'Neill, John, "McTopia: Eating Time*"*, Kumar, Krishan & Bann, Stephen (Ed) *Utopias and the Millennium* Reaktion Books Ltd, 1993, p132

13) Tappe, Anselm, *Guy Debord*, Univ. of California Press, 1999, p6-7

14) Tappe, Anselm, Op.cit, p34

15) Tappe, Anselm, Op.cit, p40

16) Stallabrass, Julian. Op.cit, p241

17) Stallabrass, Julian. Op.cit, p252

18) Stallabrass, Julian. Op.cit, p253

19) Roberts, John. "Domestic Squabble" in *Who's Afraid of Red, White and Blue?* Burrows, David (ed), University of Central England, Birmingham, Article Press, 1998, p46

20) Roberts, Op cit, p50

21) Debord,Guy *Society of the Spectacle*, Rebel Press 1987, paragraph 196

22) Buck-Morss, Susan, "Dream World of Mass Culture", *The Dialectics of Seeing: Walter Benjamin and the Arcades Project* MIT Press 1991, p268

23) Buck-Morss, Susan. Op.cit, p260

24) Buck-Morss, Susan. Op.cit, p273

25) Benjamin, Walter. "Dream City and Dream House, Dreams of the Future, Anthropological Nihilism, Jung" *The Arcades Project* trans. Howard Eiland and Kevin McLaughlin, London and Cambridge, Ma: Harvard University Press 1999, K2,3, p391-2

(26) Harris, Mark. *"The press release & alternative spaces", Who's Afraid of Red, White and Blue?* Burrows, David (ed), University of Central England, Birmingham, Article Press, 1998, p67-8

27) Stallabrass, Julian. Op.cit, p69

28) Adorno, Theodor and Horkheimer, Max. "The Culture Industry", Adorno, Theodor *The Culture Industry: Selected Essays on Mass Culture* Rouledge 1999, p38

29) Adorno, Theodor and Horkheimer, Max. Op cit, p39-41

30) Buchloh, Benjamin, "Cargo and Cult: The Displays of Thomas Hirschhorn", *Artforum, Nov,. 2001*, p173

31) Beech, Dave and Roberts, John. "Tolerating Impurities: An Ontology, Genealogy and Defence of Philistinism", *New Left Review no.227 Jan/Feb 1998*, p130.

32) Beech, Dave and Roberts, John. Op.cit, p160.

33) Stallabrass, Julian. Op.cit, p123

34) Quinn, Malcolm "The Legions of the Blind: the Philistine and Cultural Studies", Beech and Roberts (eds.) *The Philistine Controversy* Verso 2002, p260

35) Quinn, Malcolm. Op.cit, p271.

36) Kumar, Krishan. "The End of Socialism? The End of Utopia? The End of History?" Kumar, Krishan & Bann, Stephen (Eds). *Utopias and the Millennium* 1993 Reaktion Books Ltd. Harvey, David "Spaces of Hope" University of California Press 2000. p75

37) Kumar, Krishan. Op.cit, p79-80

38) Harvey, David *Spaces of Hope* University of California Press 2000, p254-5

39) Nesbit, Molly. Obrist, Hans Ulrich. and Tiravanija, Tirkrit. "Meeting Immanueal Wallerstein, "Utopia Station"" *50th Venice Biennale exhibition catalogue*, 2003 p369

40) Roberts, John. "Philosophising the Everyday", *Radical Philosophy 98 Nov/Dec 1999*, p27-28

41) Bonami, Francesco. "Introduction", *Exhibition catalogue 50th Venice Biennale*, 2003

42) Image, "Utopia Station"" *50th Venice Biennale exhibition catalogue*, 2003, p387

43) Hamza, Walker. "Disguise the Limit: Thomas Hirschhorn's World Airport", *Thomas Hirschhorn: Jumbo Spoons and Big Cake The Art Institute of Chicago World Airport The Renaissance Society at The University of Chicago,* Lowitz + Sons, Chicago, 2000, p23

44) Hamza, Walker. Op.cit, p23

45) Enwezor, Okuwi. "The Black Box", *Documenta XI* Hatje Cantz 2002, p43.

46) Enwezor, Okuwi. "The Black Box", *Documenta XI* Hatje Cantz 2002, p48

47) http://www.palestinefacts.org/pf_early_palestine_name_origin.php

Essay 7

1) James, William. *The Varieties of Religious Experience*, Fontana, 1960. pp48-9

2) Elkins, James. *What Happened to Religion in Contemporary Art?* http://www.jameselkins.com/Texts/a/religion.html, 2004 pp6-8

3) Freeland, Cynthia. *Art Theory: A Very Short Introduction*, Oxford University Press, 2003 pp18-19

4) Taylor, Mark C. *Disfiguring*, Univ. of Chicago Press, 1992 pp21-33

5) Taylor, Mark C. Op.cit, pp34-45

6) Freeland, Cynthia. Op.cit, p12

7) Ward, Glen. *Postmodernism*, Hodder Headline Limited, 2003 pp169-173

8) Ward, Glen. Op.cit, pp78-80

9) Ward, Glen. Op.cit, p81

10) Benjamin, Walter. Illuminations London, 1973 pp 219-53 taken from the English translation by Zohn, Harry in Arendt, H (ed.) reproduced in Harrison, Charles nd Wood, Paul Art in theory 1900-2000 Blackwell 2003, p526

11) Benjamin, Walter, Op.cit, p527

12) Buck-Morss, Susan, "Dream World of Mass Culture", *The Dialectics of Seeing: Walter Benjamin and the Arcades Project* MIT Press 1991, p268

13) Benjamin, Walter. "Dream City and Dream House, Dreams of the Future, Anthropological Nihilism, Jung" *The Arcades Project* trans. Howard Eiland and Kevin McLaughlin, London and Cambridge, Ma: Harvard University Press 1999, K2,3, pp391-2

14) Adorno, Theodor and Horkheimer, Max."The Culture Industry", Adorno, Theodor *The Culture Industry: Selected Essays on Mass Culture* Rouledge 1999, pp38-41

15) Greenberg, Clement. "Avant-Garde and Kitsch", 1939, in *Art in Theory 1900-1990* Harrison, Charles and Wood, Paul (Eds) Blackwell, 1998 p539

16) Tappe, Anselm, *Guy Debord*, Univ. of California Press, 1999, pp6-7

17) Tappe, Anselm, Op.cit, p34

18) Tappe, Anselm, Op.cit, p40

19) Sayre, Henry. M. *The Object of Performance : the American avant-garde since 1970*. University of Chicago Press, 1992, p31

20) Newman, Michael. "Revising Modernism, Representing Postmodernism", in *Postmodernism: ICA documents* 1985 p127

21) Ward, Glen. Op.cit, pp63-76

22) Ward, Glen. Op.cit, pp84-85

23) Ward, Glen. Op.cit, p124 referencing Poster, Mark "Postmodern Virtualities" in *Futurenatural* 1996

24) Ward, Glen. Op.cit, p124

25) Enwezor, Okuwi, "The Black Box", *Documenta XI exhibition catalogue*, 2002, p47-48

26) Pavis, Patrice. "Introduction: Towards a Theory of Interculturalism in Theatre?" Pavis, Patrice. (Ed) *The Intercultural Performance Reader*. Routledge 1996 pp4-17

27) Doss, Erika. *Twentieth-Century American Art*, Oxford, 2002

28) Gomez Pena, Guillermo. *Dangerous Border Crossers: the artist talks back* Routledge 2000 p240

29) Newman, Michael. Op.cit, p113

30) Bonito Oliva, Achille. *Trans-Avantgarde International*. 1982 Stampato in Italia. English translation Gast, Dwight and Jones Gwen. pp12-54

31) Ward, Glen. Op.cit, pp187-189

32) Freeland, Cynthia. Op.cit, pp44-46

33) Freeland, Cynthia. Op.cit, p49

34) Taylor, Mark C. Op.cit, p54

35) Golding, John. *Paths to the Absolute: Mondrian, Malevich, Kandinsky, Pollock, Newman, Rothko and Still*, Thames & Hudson, 2000, p20

36) Golding, op. cit. p157

37) Golding, op. cit. p14

38) Greenberg, Clement. "Modernist Painting", 1960, in *Art in Theory 1900-1990* Harrison, Charles and Wood, Paul (Eds) Blackwell, 1998 pp774-5

39) Ward, Glen. Op.cit, pp43-44

40) Golding, op. cit. p201

41) Taylor, Mark C. Op.cit, p224-5

42) Taylor, Mark C. Op.cit, p230

43) Nesbit, Molly. Obrist, Hans Ulrich. and Tiravanija, Tirkrit. Meeting Immanueal Wallerstein, "Utopia Station", *50th Venice Biennale exhibition catalogue,* p369

44) Harvey, David *Spaces of Hope* University of California Press, 2000, p254-5

45) Roberts, John. "Philosophising the Everyday", *Radical Philosophy 98* Nov/Dec 1999, pp27-28

46) Taylor, Mark C. Op.cit, p317

47) Taylor, Mark C. Op.cit, p270

48) Ward, Glen. Op.cit, p170

49) Ward, Glen. Op.cit, pp95-97

50) Ward, Glen. Op.cit, p105

51) Ward, Glen. Op.cit, p106

52) Derrida, Jacques Chapter 1 "Faith and Knowledge: The Two Sources of "Religion" at the Limits of Reason Alone" 1996 *Acts of Religion*. New York: Routledge, 2002. p55

53) Taylor, Mark C. Op.cit, p266
54) Ward, Glen. Op.cit, p99-100
55) Taylor, Mark C. Op.cit, pp233 Bataille, Georges. *Theory of Religion* (trans. Robert Hurley (New York: Zone Books, 1989))
56) Taylor, Mark C. p236 Bataille, Georges Op.cit,
57) Taylor, Mark C. Op.cit, p267
58) Taylor, Mark C. Op.cit, pp233-240
59) Goodall, Jane. *Artaud and the Gnostic Drama* Clarendon Press Oxford, 1994 p217
60) Goodall, Jane. Op. Cit. p217 Derrida, Jacques *Writing and Difference*
61) Goodall, Jane. Op. Cit. p17
62) Derrida, Jacques, Op. Cit. p56
63) Derrida, Jacques, Op. Cit. pp40-102
64) Walsh, Brian. "Derrida and the Messiah: The Spiritual Face of Post-modernity," *http://www.thewychefamily.com/beliefs/derridaandmessiah.html*
65) Taylor, Victor E. *Para/Inquiry: Postmodern Religion and Culture* Routledge 2000. pp109-111
66) Newman, Michael. Op.cit, p141
67) Tilley, Terrence W. *Postmodern theologies: the challenge of religious diversity,* Orbis books, 1995 pp158-167
68) Stallabraas, Julian. *High Art Lite,* Verso, 1999 p3
69) Stallabraas, Julian. Op. Cit. p139
70) Stallabraas, Julian. Op. Cit. p271
71) Gomez Pena, op. cit. pp236-7
72) Gomez Pena, op. cit. p242
73) Borean, Lionello *www.plug-pray.org* 2003
74) Reitmaier, Heidi. "God, Prayer and Politics: The Work of Shilpa Gupta" *http://www.tate.org.uk/netart/blessedbandwidth/heidireitmaier.htm,* 2003
75) Reitmaier, Heidi. Op. Cit.
76) Elkins, James. Op.cit, p50 Zizek, Slavoj
77) Reitmaier, Heidi. Op. Cit.

Essay 8

1) Walsh, Brian. *Derrida and the Messiah: The Spiritual Face of Post-modernity,* *http://www.thewychefamily.com/beliefs/derridaandmessiah.html*
2) Woodhead, Linda and Heelas, Paul (ed). *Religion in Modern Times*, Blackwell 2000 p 477
3) Koerner, Joseph Leo. *Caspar David Friedrich and the subject of landscape.* Reaktion 1990 p192
4) Koerner, op. cit. p15
5) Clark , David K & Geisler, Norman L. (1990) *Apologetics in the New Age: A Christian Critique of Pantheism.* Baker p228

6) Clark , David K & Geisler, Norman L. op. cit. p229

7) Golding, John. *Paths to the Absolute: Mondrian, Malevich, Kandinsky, Pollock, Newman, Rothko and Still*, Thames & Hudson 2000 p20
8) Golding, op. cit. p157
9) Golding, op. cit. p14
10) Golding, op. cit. p116

11) Golding, op. cit. pp133-4

12) Golding, op. cit. p126

13) Golding, op. cit. p137

14) Greenberg, Clement. "Avant-Garde and Kitsch" 1939, in *Art in Theory 1900-1990* Harrison, Charles and Wood, Paul (Eds) Blackwell 1998 p539

15) Sayre, Henry. M. *The Object of Performance : the American avant-garde since 1970.* University of Chicago Press 1992, p31

16) Newman, Michael. "Revising Modernism, Representing Postmodernism", in *Postmodernism: ICA documents* 1985 p127

17) http://www.traces-cl.com/may02/warhol.htm

18) http://***www.acfnewsource.org/cgi-bin/printer.cgi?310***.

19) Padgett, Anthony. "Digital Spirituality", in Candy, Linda, Edmonds, Ernest *Explorations in Art and Technology*, 2002

20) http://www.palsolidarity.org/

21) http://philologos.org/__eb-trs/

22) Anthony Padgett "Reconciling Binary Oppositions" in *Body, Space & Technology Journal Vol 2 Number 1,* 2001
http://www.brunel.ac.uk/depts/pfa/bstjournal/2no1/journal2no1.htm

23) *Proceedings of the 8th Intenaional Conference of ISSEI (International Society for the Study of European Ideas).* 22-27 uly 2002, Aberystwyth ISBN 0-9544363-0-X

24) Broadhurst, Susan (1999) *Liminal Acts A Critical Overview of Contemporary Performance and Theory.* Cassell: London/Continuum: New York p 34

25) Derrida, Jacques (1996) 'Faith and Knowledge: The Two Sources of "Religion" at the Limits of Reason Alone' p55 in Derrida, Jacques *Acts of Religion* Routledge 2002

26) Bonito Oliva, Achille. *Trans-Avantgarde International.* 1982 Stampato in Italia. English translation Gast, Dwight and Jones Gwen. p50

27) Bonito Oliva, op. cit. p12

28) Bonito Oliva, op. cit. p54

29) Sayre, op. cit. p18

30) Taylor, Victor E. *Para/Inquiry: Postmodern Religion and Culture* Routledge 2000. pp109-111

31) Newman, op. cit. p136

32) Tilley, Terrence W. *Postmodern theologies: the challenge of religious diversity,* Orbis books, 1995 p158

33) Tilley, op. cit. p167

34) Tilley, op. cit. p158

35) Woodhead, Linda and Heelas, Paul (ed).*Religion in Modern Times,* Blackwell 2000 p494

36) Moore, Lawrence. R. *Selling God : American Religion in the Marketplace of Culture.* Oxford University Press 1994. pp270-3

37) Start, Rodney "Bringing Theory Back In",1997 in Young, Lawrence A. (ed) *Rational Choice Theory and Religion,* New York and London: Routledge 1997 in Woodhead & Heelas, op. cit. pp462-463

38) http://newsvote.bbc.co.uk/mpapps/pagetools/print/news.bbc.co.uk/1/hi/uk_politics/3122615.stm

39) Barber, Benjamin R. *Jihad vs McWorld : Terrorism's Challenge to Democracy,* Corgi 2003.

40) Pavis, Patrice. "Introduction: Towards a Theory of Interculturalism in Theatre?" Pavis, Patrice. (Ed) *The Intercultural Performance Reader.* Routledge 1996 p4

41) Pavis, op. cit. p17
42) Bharucha, Rustom. "Somebody's Other: Disorientations In The Cultural Politics Of Our Times" in Pavis, Patrice. (Ed) *The Intercultural Performance Reader* Routledge 1996 p207
43) Barker, Clive. "The Possibilities and Politics of Intercultural Penetration and Exchange". In Pavis, Patrice. (Ed) *The Intercultural Performance Reader* Routledge 1996 pp254-256
44) Barber, op.cit. pp82-83
45) Bharucha, op. cit. p206
46) http://www.rael.org/
47) http://www.theism.co.uk - or -
http://uk.geocities.com/anthonydpadgett/theeveiirevelation.html

BIBLIOGRAPHY

"Collaborating with Catastrophe" in *Apocalypse: Beauty and Horror in Contemporary Art,* London, Thames and Hudson, 2000

Adorno, Theodor and Horkheimer, Max. "The Culture Industry", Adorno, Theodor *The Culture Industry: Selected Essays on Mass Culture* Rouledge, 1999

Arata, Luis O. "In Search of Ritual Theatre: Artaud in Mexico" in *Antonin Artaud and the Modern Theater* Ed. Plunka, Gene A. Associated University Press 1994

Artaud, Antonin, "An Affective Athleticism" in *The Theater and its Double*, trans Corti, Victor, Calder Publications, 1999

Artaud, Antonin, "Seraphim's Theatre" in *The Theater and its Double*, trans Corti, Victor, Calder Publications, 1999

Artaud, Antonin, "The Theatre of Cruelty (First Manifesto)" in *The Theater and its Double*, trans Corti, Victor, Calder Publications, 1999

Artaud, Antonin, "Theatre and Cruelty" in *The Theater and its Double*, trans Corti, Victor, Calder Publications, 1999

Artaud, Antonin, "Theatre and the Plague" in *The Theater and its Double*, trans Corti, Victor, Calder Publications, 1999

Artaud, Antonin, "Two Letters on Cruelty" in *The Theater and its Double*, trans Corti, Victor, Calder Publications, 1999

Baker-White, Robert "Artaud's Legacy in the Collectivist Avant-Garde: Community and Representation in Works by Grotowski, Chaikin and Schechner" in *Antonin Artaud and the Modern Theater* Ed. Plunka, Gene A. Associated University Press 1994

Barber, Benjamin R. *Jihad vs McWorld : Terrorism's Challenge to Democracy.* London: Corgi, 2003.

Barker, Clive. "The Possibilities and Politics of Intercultural Penetration and Exchange". In Pavis, Patrice. (Ed) *The Intercultural Performance Reader* London; New York: Routledge 1996.

Beech, Dave and Roberts, John. "Tolerating Impurities: An Ontology, Genealogy and Defence of Philistinism", *New Left Review no.227 Jan/Feb 1998*

Benjamin, Walter. "Dream City and Dream House, Dreams of the Future, Anthropological Nihilism, Jung" *The Arcades Project* trans. Howard Eiland and Kevin McLaughlin, London and Cambridge, Ma: Harvard University Press 1999

Benjamin, Walter. "Dream City and Dream House, Dreams of the Future, Anthropological Nihilism, Jung", *The Arcades Project* trans. Howard Eiland and Kevin McLaughlin, London and Cambridge, Ma: Harvard University Press, 1999

Bermel, Albert "Artaud's Theatre of Cruelty" Methuen 2001

Bharucha, Rustom. "Somebody's Other: Disorientations in the cultural politics of our times". in Pavis, Patrice. (Ed) *The Intercultural Performance Reader*. London; New York: Routledge 1996.

Bois, Yve-Alain, "The Use Value of "Formless"", in Bois, Yve-Alain and Rosalind Krauss, *Formless: A User's Guide*, New York (Zone Books), 1997

Bonami, Francesco. "Introduction", *Exhibition catalogue 50th Venice Biennale*, 2003

Bonito Oliva, Achille. *Trans-Avantgarde International*. 1982 Stampato in Italia. English translation Gast, Dwight and Jones Gwen.

Broadhurst, Susan. *Liminal Acts: A Critical Overview of Contemporary Performance and Theory*. London and New York: Cassell, 1999.

Buck-Morss, Susan, "Dream World of Mass Culture", *The Dialectics of Seeing: Walter Benjamin and the Arcades Project* MIT Press 1991

Clark, David K. & Geisler, Norman L. *Apologetics in the New Age: A Christian Critique of Pantheism* Baker 1990

Clark, Katerina & Holquist, Michael, "Chapter 14: Rabelais and His World" in *Mikhael Bakhtin*, Harvard College, 1984

Collings, Matthew. *Blimey*

Cooper, Cheryl "Aporais of chora" in Hubbard, Sue & Morley, Simon *"Chora" Exhibition Booklet* 2000

Costich, Julia F. *Antonin Artaud* Twayne Publishers 1978

Debord,Guy *Society of the Spectacle*, Rebel Press 1987

Derrida, Jacques "Faith and Knowledge: The Two Sources of "Religion" at the Limits of Reason Alone" 1996 *Acts of Religion.* New York: Routledge, 2002.

Derrida, Jaques "The Theatre of Cruelty and the Closure of Representation", *Writing and Difference*, trans Alan Bass, Chicago University Press, Chicago 1978

Doss, Erika. *Twentieth-Century American Art*, Oxford, 2002

Enwezor, Okuwi, *"Interview with Thomas Hirschhorn", Thomas Hirschhorn: Jumbo Spoons and Big Cake The Art Institute of Chicago World Airport The Renaissance Society at The University of Chicago*, Lowitz + Sons, Chicago, 2000

Enwezor, Okuwi. "The Black Box", *Documenta XI* Hatje Cantz, 2002

Falconer, David. "Doctorin' the Retardis" in *Chapmanworld*

Fiat, Christopher. "The Experience of Violence in Sacrifice", *Documenta XI exhibition* catalogue (2002)

Fogle, Douglas. "A Scatological Aesthetics for the Tired of Seeing" in *Chapmanworld* Gagosian Gallery, *Unholy Libel*, 1997

Freeland, Cynthia. *Art Theory: A Very Short Introduction*, Oxford UnivPress, 2003

Goldberg, RoseLee *Performance: Live Art since the 60's* Thames and Hudson 1998

Golding, John. *Paths to the Absolute: Mondrian, Malevich, Kandinsky, Pollock, Newman, Rothko and Still*. London: Thames & Hudson, 2000.

Gomez Pena, Guillermo. *Dangerous Border Crossers: the artist talks back* Routledge, 2000

Goodall, Jane *Artaud and the Gnostic Drama* Clarendon Press Oxford 1994

Greenberg, Clement. "Avant-Garde and Kitsch" 1939, in *Art in Theory 1900-2000* Harrison, Charles and Wood, Paul (Eds) Blackwell, 2003.

Hamann, Brigitte. *Hitler's Vienna: A Dictator' Apprenticeship* Oxford University Press 1999

Hamza, Walker. "Disguise the Limit: Thomas Hirschhorn's World Airport", *Thomas Hirschhorn: Jumbo Spoons and Big Cake The Art Institute of Chicago World Airport The Renaissance Society at The University of Chicago*, Lowitz + Sons, Chicago, 2000

Harris, Mark. "The press release & alternative spaces", *Who's Afraid of Red, White and Blue?* Burrows, David (ed), University of Central England, Birmingham, Article Press, 1998

Harrison, Charles & Wood, Paul (Eds). "Part IV Introduction" in *Art in Theory 1900-1990.*

Harvey, David. *Spaces of Hope,* University of California Press, 2000

Hayman, Ronald *Artaud and After* Oxford University Press 1977

James, William. The Varieties of Religious Experience, Fontana, 1960

Kirby, Michael. "Happenings: an introduction" (1965) reprinted in *Happenings and Other Acts,* ed: Mariellen R. Sandford, Routledge, 1995

Knapp, Bettina L. *Antonin Artaud – Man of Vision* Swallow Press 1980

Koerner, Joseph Leo. *Caspar David Friedrich and the subject of landscape*. London: Reaktion 1990

Kumar, Krishan. "The End of Socialism? The End of Utopia? The End of History?" (Ed) Kumar, Krishan & Bann, Stephen *Utopias and the Millennium* 1993 Reaktion Books Ltd. Harvey, David "Spaces of Hope" University of California Press 2000

Moore, Lawrence. R. *Selling God : American Religion in the Marketplace of Culture*. New York: Oxford University Press 1994.

Nesbit, Molly. Obrist, Hans Ulrich. and Tiravanija, Tirkrit. "Meeting Immanueal Wallerstein, "Utopia Station"", *50th Venice Biennale exhibition catalogue*, 2003

Newman, Michael. *"*Revising Modernism, Representing Postmodernism*"*, 1985, in Appignanesi, Lisa (Ed). *Postmodernism: ICA documents* London: Free Association Books 1989.

O'Neill, John, "McTopia: Eating Time", Kumar, Krishan & Bann, Stephen (Ed) *Utopias and the Millennium* Reaktion Books Ltd, 1993

Padgett, Anthony "Digital Spirituality" in Candy, Linda, Edmonds, Ernest *Explorations in Art and Technology*, London: Springer-Verlag 2002.

Pavis, Patrice. "Introduction: Towards a Theory of Interculturalism in Theatre?" Pavis, Patrice. (Ed) *The Intercultural Performance Reader*. London; New York: Routledge 1996.

Plunka, Gene A. "Antonin Artaud: The Suffering Shaman of the Modern Theatre" in *Antonin Artaud and the Modern Theater* Ed. Plunka, Gene A. Associated University Press 1994

Quinn, Malcolm "The Legions of the Blind: the Philistine and Cultural Studies", Beech and Roberts (eds.) *The Philistine Controversy* Verso 2002

Roberts, John. "Domestic Squabble", *Who's Afraid of Red, White and Blue?* Burrows, David (ed), University of Central England, Birmingham, Article Press, 1998

Sayre, Henry. M. *The Object of Performance : the American avant-garde since 1970*. Chicago: University of Chicago Press 1992

Stallabrass, Julian. *High Art Lite*, Verso 1999

Start, Rodney "Bringing Theory Back In*"*,1997 in Young, Lawrence A. (ed) *Rational Choice Theory and Religion*, New York and London: Routledge 1997 in Woodhead, Linda and Heelas, Paul (ed). *Religion in Modern Times*, Oxford: Blackwell 2000.

Susan Sontag, "Approaching Artaud", introduction to *Antonin Artuad, Selected Writings*, trans.Helen Weaver(Berkeley:Univesity of California Press, 1976)

Tappe, Anselm, *Guy Debord*, Univ. of California Press, 1999

Taylor, Mark C. *Disfiguring*, Univ. of Chicago Press, 1992

Taylor, Victor E. *Para/Inquiry: Postmodern Religion and Culture*. London & New York: Routledge 2000.

Terrence W. Tilley *Postmodern theologies: the challenge of religious diversity*, New York: Orbis books, 1995

Tilley, Terrence W. *Postmodern Theologies: The Challenge Of Religious Diversity*, New York: Orbis books, 1995

Ward, Glen. *Postmodernism*, Hodder Headline Limited, 2003

Woodhead, Linda and Heelas, Paul (ed). *Religion in Modern Times*, Oxford: Blackwell 2000.

Young, Iris Marion "The Ideal of Community and the Politics of Difference" in *Feminism/Postmodernism* Ed. Nicholson, Linda J. Routledge 1990

JOURNALS/PERIODICALS

Anon, "Disasters of War II", *Art Forum International*, vol 39, no 1, Sept 2000

Attias, Laurie, "Galerie Templon", *Sculpture*, vol 17, no 9, Nov 1998

Avgikas, Jan, "Gagosian Gallery", *Art Forum International*, vol 36, Dec 1997

Battray, Fiona, "The Art of Shopping", *Blueprint*, no 164, Sept 1999

Bevan, Roger, "Chapman World – How far can they go?", *Art Newspaper*, vol 7, May 1996

Bevan, Roger, "Will the Turner Prize jury summon Jake and Dinos Chapman?", *Art Newspaper*, vol 7, June 1996

Birnbaum, Daniel, "Andrehn Schiptjenho", *Art Forum International*, vol 33, Summer 1995

Brown, Neal, "Victoria Miro Gallery", *Art and Text*, no 50, Jan 1995

Buchloh, Benjamin, "Cargo and Cult: The Displays of Thomas Hirschhorn," *Artforum, Nov. 2001*

Castelluci, Romeo," The Animal Being on Stage", Perfomance Research (5)2,

Chapman, Dinos, "Gender is an Organic Superstition", *MAKE: The Magazine of Womens' Art*, Aug/Sept 1996

Chapman, Jake & Chapman, Dinos, "Florence Biennnale", *Flash Art (International Edition)*, no 192, Jan/Feb 1997

Chapman, Jake & Chapman, Dinos, "Jake and Dinos Chapman's Top Ten", *Art Forum International*, vol 36, no 9, May 1998

Chapman, Jake & Chapman, Dinos, "Project", *Art and Text*, no 51, May 1995

Chapman, Jake & Chapman, Dinos, "Young British Art: A Photo Romance", *Modern Painters*, vol 13, no 2, Summer 2000

Chapman, Jake, "Fuckface", *Art and Design*, vol 12, Sept/Oct 1997

Collings, Matthew, "Cadmium Yellow Deep", *Modern Painters*, vol 9, Summer 1996,

Corris, Michael, "Victoria Miro Gallery", *Art Forum International*, vol 31, Summer 1993

Grayford, Martin, "Shock Value", *Modern Painters*, vol 13, no 3, Autumn 2000

Green, David & Lowry, Joanna, "Zygotic Exposure", *Creative Camera*, no 341, Aug/Sept 1996

Hall, Charles, "Show Hide Show", *Arts Review*, vol 43, Aug 9 & 23, 1991

Harris, Mark, "ICA", *Art in America*, vol 84, Oct 1996

Hayt, Elizabeth, "Exhibit", *Art Text*, no 60, Feb/April 1998

Heartney, Eleanor, "New York Exhibit", *Art in America*, vol 85, Nov 1997, p120

Herbstreuth, Peter "Disasters of War" *Kunstforum International*, no152,Oct/Dec 2000

Hilty, Greg, "Shock, Boredom, Modernism", *Art Press*, no 234, April 1998, p38-42

Jacques, Alison, "Victoria Miro Gallery", *Flash Art (International Edition)*, no 180, Jan/Feb 1995

Jones, Jonathan, *Frieze* 1999 Issue 47

Legge, Elizabeth, "Now Then", *Canadian Art*, vol 18, no 1, Spring 2001

Maloney, Martin, "The Chapman Brothers", *Flash Art* (International Edition), no 186, Jan/Feb 1996

Ramkalawon, Jennifer, "Disasters of War", *Print Quarterly*, vol 18 no 1, March 2001

Roberts, John. "Philosophising the Everyday", *Radical Philosophy 98 Nov/Dec 1999*

Rosenblum, Robert, "ICA", *Art Forum International*, vol 35, Sept 1996

Schwendener, Martha, "Gagosian", *New Art Examiner*, vol 25, Dec 97/Jan 98

Sladen, Mark, "The Body in Question", *Art Monthly*, no 191, 1995

Sladen, Mark, "Vice and Versatility", *Art Press*, no 214, June 1996

Smyth, C, "Art Monthly", no 238, 2000
Usherwood, Paul, "The Cauldron", *Art Monthly,* no 198, 1996
Withers, Rachel, "Exhibit", *Art Forum International*, vol 37, no 4, Dec 1998
Worsdale, Godfrey, "Victoria Miro Gallery", *Art Monthly*, no 180, Oct 1994

WEBSITES

Borean, Lionello www.plug-pray.org
Carroll, Pete *The Magick of Chaos* http://www.chaosmatrix.org
Elkins, James "What Happened to Religion in Contemporary Art?"
Frangi, Giuseppe "Warhol's Madonna" http://www.traces-cl.com/may02/warhol.htm 2002
Gupta, Shilpa www.blessed-bandwidth.net
http://newsvote.bbc.co.uk/mpapps/pagetools/print/news.bbc.co.uk/1/hi/uk_politics/31 22615.stm
http://www.geocities.com/onemansmind/hg/Aryan.html 2001
http://www.jameselkins.com/Texts/a/religion.html 2004
http://www.palestinefacts.org/pf_early_palestine_name_origin.php
http://www.qibla-cola.com/
http://www.thewychefamily.com/beliefs/derridaandmessiah.html
Padgett,Anthony http://uk.geocities.com/anthonydpadgett/theeveiirevelation.html 2004
Padgett, Anthony. http://www.theism.co.uk 1999-2004
Reitmaier, Heidi. "God, Prayer and Politics: The Work of Shilpa Gupta" 2003 http://www.tate.org.uk/netart/blessedbandwidth/heidireitmaier.htm,
Tate Magazine, Issue 3, http://www.tate.org.uk/magazine/issue3/michaellandy.htm
The International Solidarity Movement http://www.palsolidarity.org/
The Raelian Movement, http://www.rael.org/
Walsh, Brian J. "Derrida and the Messiah: The Spiritual Face of Postmodernity." *Regeneration Quarterly* 5 (spring 1999): 29-33. *(Posted 10/19/2001)*
Walsh, Brian. "Derrida and the Messiah: The Spiritual Face of Post-modernity",

NEWSPAPER ARTICLES

Aidin, Rose, *Saturday Telegraph Magazine*, 2 September 2000
Barber, L, "Brothers in Art", *Observer*, 1999
Barber, Lynn, *Life: the Observer Magazine,* 28 March 1999
Berens, Jessica, *Tatler* September 2000 Vol.295 No.9
Coomer, Martin, *Time Out* April 7-14
Hall, James, "Brush with Death", *Guardian,* 1994
Jackson, A, "Charm Offensive", *Times*, 1997
Januszczak, W, "It's just not grim enough", *Sunday Times*, 2000
Levin, Kim. "More Is More", *Village Voice, November 27-December 3*, 2002
Milner, Catherine, *The Sunday Telegraph,* 6 February 200
O'Sullivan, C, "Dedicated followers of Fascism", *Observer,* 1995
Popham, Peter, "Jake and Dinos and All their…", *Independent on Sunday,* 1996
Searle, Adrian, *Guardian* March 23 1999
Tressider, M, "Brilliant Bad Boys", *Guardian,* 1995
Vallely, P, "The Brothers Grim", *Independent,* 2000
Walsh, N.P., "An Artist's Home is His Studio", *Observer,* 2000

INDEX

www.ingramcontent.com/pod-product-compliance
Lightning Source LLC
Chambersburg PA
CBHW020351270326
41926CB00007B/391